ge

Student Support Materials for

AQA AS Sociology

Unit 1
Families and Households

Authors: Martin Holborn and Liz Steel

Series editor: Peter Langley

Published by Collins Education
An imprint of HarperCollins Publishers
77-85 Fulham Palace Road
Hammersmith
London
W6 8JB

Browse the complete Collins Education catalogue at
www.collinseducation.com

10 9 8 7 6 5 4 3 2 1

ISBN 978-0-00-741598-4

British Library Cataloguing in Publication Data.

A catalogue record for this publication is available from the British Library.

Project editor: Sarah Vittachi

Design and typesetting by Hedgehog Publishing Limited

Cover Design by Angela English

Production by Simon Moore

Printed and bound by L.E.G.O. S.p.A Italy

Indexed by Indexing Specialists (UK) Ltd

Acknowledgements

Every effort has been made to contact the holders of copyright material, but if any have been inadvertently overlooked the publishers will be pleased to make the necessary arrangements at the first opportunity.

p15, fig 2, source: Office for National Statistics; p29m tables 6 and 7, source: General Household Survey, Office for National Statistics; p32, table 8, source: General Household Survey, Office for National Statistics; p34, table 9, source: ONS (2006) Social Focus on Ethnic Groups (no longer available for checking); p37, table 10, source: : ONS Social Trends 2009; p38, fig 7, source: ONS Social Trends 2009; p40, fig 8, source: www.statistics.gov.uk; p46, table 12, source: The British Social Attitudes Survey; p47, table 13, source: ONS Time Use Survey 2005; p50, fig 10, source: Home Office (2010) Crime in England and Wales 2009/10; p58, fig 11, source: Social Trends 2009; p59, fig 12, source: Social Trends 2009; p63, table 17, source: Social Trends 2009; p66, fig 14, source: www.statistics.gov.uk

The family and social structure 4–27

Defining the family; Functionalist theories of the family; Marxist theories of the family; Feminist theories of the family; New Right perspectives on the family; The family and social change; Changing family structures; The family and modernity; Postmodernity and the family; Social policy and the family

Family diversity 28–37

The growth of family diversity; Family diversity and lone parenthood; Ethnicity and family diversity; Diversity and the decline of conventional families

Relationships 38–45

Changing patterns of marriage and cohabitation; Divorce and marital breakdown; The changing life course

Gender, power and the family 46–51

Conjugal roles, housework and childcare; Conjugal roles, power and emotion work; Domestic violence and abuse

Childhood 52–57

The social construction of childhood; Changing childhood; Contemporary perspectives on childhood

Demographic changes and the family 58–67

Demography and the birth rate; The death rate; Migration; The ageing population

Exam practice 68–83

Glossary 84–90

Index 92–93

Defining the family

At first sight it seems easy to define the family. Most people could easily identify whom they consider to be members of their family. Usually this will include their mother and father, brothers and sisters, any children and possibly less close relatives such as grandparents, aunts and uncles. We are connected to these individuals either through blood (genetic) links or through marriage. Seeing the family in this way is a commonsense definition of the family, and this was the starting point for the **functionalist** sociologist George Peter Murdock (1949).

Murdock defined the family as 'a social group characterised by common residence, economic cooperation and reproduction. It includes adults of both sexes, at least two of whom maintain a socially approved sexual relationship, and one or more children, own or adopted, of the sexually cohabiting adults'.

Murdock studied 250 societies and claimed the family, as defined above, was present in all of them. He therefore saw it as a **universal** institution (found in all societies) which was necessary for the smooth functioning and survival of any society.

Murdock's definition only includes members of the **nuclear family**, which consists of two generations, parents and their immature offspring. The **extended family** also includes relations by blood or marriage from other generations (e.g. grandparents) and the siblings of parents (aunts and uncles of the children) as well as more distant relatives such as cousins.

Is the family universal?

A problem with Murdock's views is that a number of societies have very different domestic arrangements to those he describes. These examples may suggest that the family is not universal.

The Nayar

Research by Kathleen Gough (1959) into the **Nayar** of southern India found that wives did not live with the man they married (their *tali* husband) and instead had several visiting husbands (*sandbanham* husbands). Sandbanham husbands slept with a wife but did not live with her permanently. These husbands (who were usually warriors) would arrive at their wife's house at night but would have to leave if another man had arrived first and had left his spear outside the house. Each man could have several wives. In terms of Murdock's definition this society did not possess a family since fathers did not live with their children.

Matrifocal families

Research in the Caribbean, parts of central America and the USA has found that a significant proportion of households do not contain an adult male. These female-headed or **matrifocal families** appear to be an exception to Murdock's belief that the nuclear family is universal.

The sociologist Gonzalez (1970) found that matrifocal families are a well-organized social group which is well adapted to living in poverty. The mothers who head these families often get strong support from female relatives that helps them to cope with raising children. Yanina Sheeran

(1993) believes that the **female carer-core**, consisting of a mother and her children, is the basic family unit. She argues that this family unit is universal. However, a problem with this definition is the existence of male-headed households, where a single father raises children.

Gay and lesbian families

Gay families do not conform to Murdock's definition because they do not contain adults of both sexes and in some societies the sexual relationship involved might not be approved throughout society. They might, however, include children from a previous heterosexual relationship, or children who have been adopted or produced through new reproductive technologies. Sydney Callahan (1997) believes that gay or lesbian households with children should be regarded as families.

In 2005 in the UK, **civil partnerships** (which involve similar legal rights and obligations to marriage) for gay and lesbian couples were legalized, implying that gay and lesbian relationships are now socially accepted and their households should be regarded as families.

Conclusion – ideology and the family

As we have seen, there are a range of problems with Murdock's definition of the family. These are summarized below.

Definition	Problem
Common residence	Husband and wife do not always cohabit, e.g. the Nayar
Sexually approved adult relationships	Lack of agreement on approved relationships
Contains adults of both sexes	Lesbian/gay and matrifocal familes do not conform
Contains one or more children	Child-free couples can be seen as a family

Diana Gittins (1993) concludes that there is no single family type that is found in all societies. The form which families and households take varies widely, so it is not possible to produce a definition of the family which fits all societies. Nevertheless, all societies have intimate relationships and parents caring for their children.

Definitions of the family vary and are influenced by ideological differences.

- **New Right** thinkers tend to support narrow definitions which see nuclear families based around married couples as the only true family type (see p 14). Many supporters of this viewpoint see the family as an institution under threat.
- Increasing **family diversity** (see p 28) suggests that in countries such as the UK no one type of family is the norm any longer. Supporters of increasing diversity such as the Rapoports (1982) see this as a good thing because it gives people more freedom to choose how to live their lives. From this viewpoint, any household with intimate relationships can be seen as a family.

Examiners' notes

The issue of matrifocal families is also important for discussing family diversity and particularly ethnic diversity.

Examiners' notes

The growth and acceptance of gay and lesbian families in some societies is an important aspect of change in families and in society in general.

Table 1
Problems with Murdock's definition of the family

Examiners' notes

The term 'the family' is sometimes used to describe groups living together, usually a nuclear family living under the one roof, but can also be used to describe groups related by blood or marriage who do not live together; for example extended families when the whole family does not share a single residence. Make sure that you specify whether you are describing a co-resident group (or **household**) or not when writing about family types. (A household is a group of people who live together in a single dwelling.)

Functionalist theories of the family

The functionalist perspective

Functionalists see society as an interrelated whole. To functionalists, every institution in society performs one or more important **functions** or jobs and the sociologist has to determine what these functions are. They assume that institutions help society to run smoothly like a well-oiled machine. Functionalist theories of the family therefore look for the positive benefits and functions the family performs for all societies.

George Peter Murdock – the universal functions of the family

As discussed in on p 4, Murdock (1949) believed that the nuclear family was a **universal** institution vital to the well-being of all societies. From his study of 250 societies he identified four functions of the family:

1. The **sexual function**. The family prevents disruption to society by limiting sexuality to monogamous relationships, preventing the conflict that might otherwise result from sexual desire.
2. The **reproductive function**. The family ensures the reproduction of a new generation vital for the survival of society.
3. The **economic function**. The family acts as an economic unit ensuring the survival of its members by providing food and shelter.
4. The **educational function**. The family provides a stable environment in which children can be socialized into the culture of their society.

Talcott Parsons – the basic and irreducible functions of the family

Parsons (1959, 1965) studied American society and found that even though the family had lost some functions (see below) it retained two 'basic and irreducible functions':

1. **Primary socialization**. The family was the only institution in which primary socialization (the first and most important stage of socialization) could take place effectively so that children would internalize the norms and values of their society.
2. **Stabilization of adult personalities**. In Western societies the **isolated nuclear family** gets little support from **extended kinship networks**. The stress of the competitive world of work for the husband can be counterbalanced by the warmth and security offered by the nuclear family, and within the family adults can act out the childish elements in their personalities. This helps to stabilize their personalities.

Talcott Parsons – changing family structure

Parsons believed that the structure of the family changes to fit the needs of different types of society.

In **pre-industrial societies** the **extended family** was the norm. Most people worked in agriculture and the extended family worked the land together. The **nuclear family** of parents and children developed in industrial society where it was necessary because:

1. Industry required a geographically mobile workforce which could move to where new factories were being built. This was difficult to achieve with large extended families.

2. A **socially mobile** workforce was also necessary. In extended families, **status** was largely **ascribed** (given by birth) with the eldest males having high status. This could cause problems if younger males had a higher **achieved status** because they had a better job. Nuclear families without extended kin avoided this problem.

Talcott Parsons – changing functions of the family

Parsons argued that as society changes, the family loses some of its functions. In pre-industrial times it carried out many functions but in industrial society specialist institutions take over some of these functions. This process is called structural differentiation.

For example, health care and support for the family used to be the responsibility of the family. Now the welfare state has taken over much of the responsibility.

Criticisms of functionalism

The functionalist view of the family has been heavily criticized for being outdated and for presenting an overly optimistic view of family life. Criticisms include the following:

Functionalist view	Criticism
Family has a unique functional role	Some societies don't have traditional families
Family is functional for all members	Ignores 'dark side', e.g. domestic violence, sexual abuse
Family unit benefits all members	Feminists argue men benefit more than women
Families and society benefit from men being main breadwinners and women main carers	Feminists view this as patriarchal and sexist
Dominant family type has shifted from extended to nuclear	Ignores evidence of non-dominance of extended family in the pre-industrial era, and decline of nuclear family and increasing family diversity
Nuclear family best adapted to modern society	Postmodernists argue there are many viable alternatives

Essential notes

The functionalist Ronald Fletcher (1966) believed the family has developed some new functions such as acting as a unit of consumption – goods are bought for families as a whole. Fletcher also believed that the family retains important functions in education and health, supplementing and supporting the job done by schools, doctors and hospitals.

Examiners' notes

All the main perspectives (Marxism, feminism, the New Right and postmodernism) can be used to criticize functionalism. When revising it is important to identify similarities and differences between the main perspectives. The table of criticisms is not exhaustive; as you work through the material think about other ways that functionalism can be criticized.

Table 2
Criticisms of the functionalist view of family

Marxist theories of the family

Introduction to Marxism

According to Marx (1818–1883) and Engels (1820–1895) power in society largely stemmed from wealth. In particular, those who owned the **means of production** (the things needed to produce other things such as land, capital, machinery and labour power) formed a powerful **ruling class**. They were able to exploit the **subject class** (those who did not own the means of production) and therefore had to work for the ruling class.

Economic systems

According to Marx, society passed through several periods in which different economic systems or **modes of production** were dominant. In each of these there was a different ruling class and subject class. In the latest stage, **capitalist society**, the ruling class were wealthy factory owners (the **bourgeoisie**) and the subject class were the **working-class** employees (the proletariat). In capitalism the proletariat was exploited by the bourgeoisie because they were not paid the full value of their work since the bourgeoisie kept some **surplus value** or profit.

The economic base and superstructure

The power of the bourgeoisie derived from their ownership of the means of production. The means of production formed the **economic base** or infrastructure of society. Because they controlled the economic base the bourgeoisie were able to control the other, non-economic institutions of society (which make up the **superstructure**) such as the media, government, religion and the family.

Examiners' notes

It is important to use technical terms from Marxist theory (such as means of production) when answering exam questions.

Examiners' notes

The economic base/ superstructure model of society is very useful for explaining why Marxists see the family as being shaped by the interests of the ruling class.

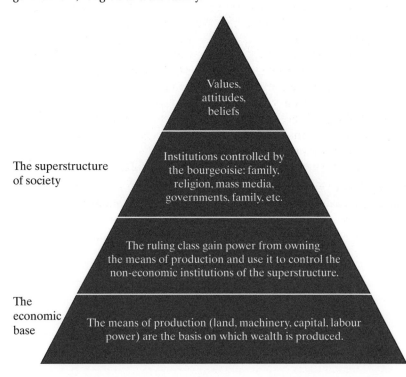

The superstructure of society

Values, attitudes, beliefs

Institutions controlled by the bourgeoisie: family, religion, mass media, governments, family, etc.

The ruling class gain power from owning the means of production and use it to control the non-economic institutions of the superstructure.

The economic base

The means of production (land, machinery, capital, labour power) are the basis on which wealth is produced.

Fig 1
A Marxist model of society

Marxist perspectives on the family

- Engels (1884) argued that the family developed so that men could be certain of the paternity of children, with marriage allowing them to control women's sexuality. This enabled them to be more confident that they were passing their property down to their biological offspring.
- Zaretsky (1976) sees the family as a prop to the capitalist system. The unpaid **domestic labour** of housewives supports future generations of workers at no cost to capitalist employers. The family consumes the commodities produced by capitalist companies, helping the bourgeoisie to make profits. It also provides comfort to **alienated** workers enabling them to carry on working.
- Poulantzas (1969) sees the family as part of the superstructure of society. He describes it as part of the **ideological state apparatus**, which is controlled by the bourgeoisie and used to create values, attitudes and beliefs which support the capitalist system and the position of the ruling class.
- The view of Poulantzas is supported by David Cooper (1972), who sees the family as 'an ideological conditioning device' in which children learn to conform to authority so they will become cooperative and easily exploited workers.

Criticisms of Marxism

The Marxist view of the family has been criticized from a variety of viewpoints.

- Some modern evidence contradicts the view that the family only developed after the herding of animals was introduced.
- Zaretsky has been criticized for exaggerating the extent to which the family can be an escape from alienating work since the family can also be characterized by cruelty, neglect and violence.
- Some families are anti-capitalist and socialize their children into beliefs which are critical of the ruling class.
- Feminists criticize Marxists for neglecting the exploitation of women, postmodernists criticize them for ignoring the variety of family types present in society today and functionalists believe that Marxists ignore the beneficial functions of the family for society.

Strengths of Marxism

Marxism is useful for highlighting the importance of economic influences on family life and because it raises the possibility that the family as an institution benefits some social groups (higher classes) more than others.

Examiners' notes

Make sure that you learn the views on the family of at least three Marxists.

Examiners' notes

It can also be useful to discuss Marxist feminist views of the family (see p 12) which are quite similar to Marxist views.

Essential notes

The postmodern view of family life draws attention to the way in which Marxists assume that the nuclear family is still the norm. In fact increasing **family diversity** (see p 28) raises doubts about the possibility of making any generalizations about the role of families in society.

Feminist theories of the family

The basic principles of feminism

There are several different types of feminist theory, but all of them share certain characteristics in common:

- There is a fundamental division in society between men and women.
- That women are to some extent exploited by men.
- That society is male-dominated or **patriarchal**. Literally, patriarchal means 'rule by the father' but is used by feminists to indicate that men have more power than women and the interests of men largely shape how societies run.

These theories are also all critical of existing sociology, arguing that it has a pro-male bias. They call male-dominated sociology '**malestream**' sociology, claiming that most sociology is written by men, about men and for men. For example, most early studies of the family used all-male samples and paid little attention to women's roles and work within the family such as the role of mother and the work of mothering or housework.

From the early 1970s feminist thinking became more influential in sociology and this was reflected in a growing number of studies of the family from a feminist viewpoint. However, there are important differences between the perspectives of different feminists.

The table below summarizes three of the main varieties of feminism that have been applied to the study of the family.

	Radical feminism	Marxist feminism	Liberal feminism
Society is controlled by:	Men	Men and capitalists (the wealthy ruling class)	Largely by men who have more power than women, but women do have some power
Society is defined as:	Patriarchal (male dominated)	Patriarchal	Basically democratic but it is also sexist with discrimination against women
Who benefits from inequalities in society?	Men	Men in general, but ruling-class men in particular. Working-class men get wives to work for them (e.g. housework) but the ruling class exploits women both as workers and wives	Nobody. Gender stereotypes mean that men miss out on the private side of life (e.g. raising children) and women miss out in public life, e.g. paid employment

Main ideas behind the theory:	Women are dominated by men due to biology (women give birth, men are stronger) and men use violence or **ideology** (distorted beliefs) to control women	Men's financial power keeps women in their place. Women do more unpaid work (e.g. as mothers and housewives) and receive lower wages making them financially dependent on men	Socialization into gender roles (e.g. differences in boys' and girls' toys) and sexist discrimination (e.g. in the labour market) restrict women's opportunities
Solutions to the exploitation of women:	Radical change (e.g. a female-dominated society or separation of the sexes)	Communist revolution or more economic equality to get rid of men's financial power	Gradual reform. Getting rid of sexism in socialization (e.g. children's books) and the use of language. Laws against discrimination (e.g. Equal Pay Act)
Criticisms:	The idea of patriarchy is too broad and doesn't really explain why women are exploited. It exaggerates the extent of **inequality** and fails to take account of the development of greater equality	Places too much emphasis on economic factors	Lacks a theory of the underlying causes of inequality

Table 3
Types of feminism

Essential notes

Another criticism that has been made of all these varieties of feminism is that the concept of patriarchy does not really explain gender inequality but only describes it.

Examiners' notes

Remember that the different perspectives can be used to criticize and evaluate one another.

Essential notes

Difference feminism has much in common with postmodernism.

Difference feminism

The three feminist perspectives outlined above all tend to see women as a single group who share interests and are all equally exploited. However, **difference feminism** emphasizes that women are not one single, united group but rather have a variety of interests.

Black feminists, for example, stress the importance of racial/**ethnic** differences between women while other difference feminists emphasize differences in **class**, age or nationality. Difference feminists point out that not all women are equally exploited.

Essential notes

Evidence of **domestic violence** and sexual abuse perpetrated by men can be used to support radical feminism.

Essential notes

Some studies in the sections on conjugal roles and power in households (pp 46–49) can be used to support Marxist feminist views.

Examiners' notes

You can develop these criticisms in more detail by discussing how functionalist, Marxist and postmodern theories differ from them.

Feminist perspectives and the family
Radical feminism and the family

Radical feminists believe that the family plays a major role in maintaining the oppression of women in a patriarchal, male-dominated society.

Germaine Greer (2000) argues that even in marriage today women remain subservient to their husbands. She believes that single women are generally happier than married women and this is reflected in the high number of divorces instigated by women. Greer claims that wives are much more likely to suffer physical and sexual abuse than husbands, and daughters are often victims of sexual abuse by male relatives within the family.

Marxist feminism and the family

Marxist feminists believe that the family benefits the capitalist system and in doing so exploits women.

- Margaret Benston (1972) claims that wives are used to produce and rear cheap labour for employers. The childcare they provide is unpaid, and they also help to maintain their husbands as workers at no cost to employers.
- Fran Ansley (1972) believes that wives suffer as a result of the frustration experienced by their husbands in the **alienating** work that they do for capitalists.

Liberal feminism and the family

The liberal feminist Jennifer Somerville (2000) believes that women are still disadvantaged in families, but she criticizes radical and Marxist feminists for failing to accept that progress has been made in some ways.

- Women now have much more choice about whether to marry, whether they take paid work when married and whether they stay married.
- There is now greater equality within marriage and greater sharing of the responsibility for paid and unpaid work and childcare.
- Most women still value relationships with men.

However, she agrees there are still inequalities within marriage that need to be tackled through pragmatic reform. For example, better childcare is needed for working parents, and more flexibility is needed in jobs so that both men and women can contribute fully to family life.

Criticisms of radical, Marxist and liberal feminist perspectives on the family

All these perspectives have been criticized for:

- Exaggerating the exploitation of women within the family.
- Largely failing to acknowledge the increasing equality between men and women.
- Oversimplifying by taking little account of differences in the circumstances of different groups of women.
- In particular, not taking account of class, ethnic and age differences.
- Ignoring examples where men are victims of abuse in families.

Functionalists criticize them for failing to acknowledge the positive contribution of the family to society.

Postmodernists criticize them for failing to acknowledge the extent to which society and family life have changed.

Difference feminism and the family

This perspective recognizes that there is increasing family diversity today and women may not be equally exploited in all family types. For example, many women are lone parents and as such cannot be exploited by a cohabiting man. There are also differences in gender relationships in families from different ethnic backgrounds.

- Nicholson (1997) believes that women are often better off outside traditional families and all types of family and household should be socially accepted because they suit women in different circumstances.
- Calhoun (1997) points out that women cannot be exploited by men in lesbian families. She believes that there is increasing choice in family life, and gay and lesbian families are examples of '**chosen families**'.

Criticisms of difference feminism

Difference feminism is not as easy to criticize as other forms of feminism because it recognizes differences in family life. However, other types of feminists criticize it for losing sight of continuing inequalities between men and women within the family.

The contribution of feminism to understanding the family

Despite the criticisms of feminism it has contributed to the sociology of the family in a number of ways:

- It has shown that the family may benefit some members, particularly adult males, more than others.
- It has highlighted the existence of violence, abuse and exploitation within the family.
- Feminists have conducted research into areas of family life which have either been neglected or not been studied before. These include conjugal roles, motherhood, pregnancy, childbirth and childcare.
- It has analyzed the contribution of housework to the economy.

Feminism has therefore helped to correct the masculine bias in the previous sociology of the family and to illuminate family life from the perspective of women.

Examiners' notes

This study can be linked to evidence of increasing family diversity (p 28).

Examiners' notes

Studies of the growth of gay and lesbian families are very useful for answering a wide range of questions about the family, including those on theories of the family, threats to the family, increasing diversity and the direction of social change affecting the family.

Examiners' notes

The highest marks for evaluation tend to be given to those who have a balanced discussion – that is, they look at both the strengths and weaknesses of a perspective, approach or study.

New Right perspectives on the family

Introduction to the New Right

New Right views are associated with the ideas and policies of political parties. In Britain, New Right thinking influenced the policies of the Conservative governments of Margaret Thatcher and John Major between 1979 and 1997.

The New Right's perspective strongly supports **free-market** capitalism. It believes that the state should intervene as little as possible in the economy, leaving **private enterprise** to generate wealth. From this viewpoint **competition** benefits consumers and society as a whole by driving down the price of goods while driving up the quality. New Right thinkers see markets as based on choice and believe they encourage individual liberty.

The New Right and the family

However, New Right theorists do not see choice and liberty as being so important in terms of family life. Instead, they see traditional **nuclear families** as the cornerstone of stability in society. They favour traditional families for the following reasons:

- They see them as encouraging self-reliance – family members help each other rather than relying on the state.
- This helps to reduce state expenditure on welfare (for example, for lone parents).
- They see families as encouraging shared moral values and believe they are the best way to pass down morality to children.

Unlike functionalists, New Right thinkers do not believe that the family is a stable institution, able to carry out its functions for individuals and society as a whole. Instead they see it as increasingly unstable, leading to an increase in social problems.

The New Right and policies

When Margaret Thatcher was in power, some policies were introduced to try to support the traditional nuclear family of a married couple and children. For example, in 1988 taxation was changed so that cohabiting couples could no longer claim greater allowances than married couples.

Pamela Abbott and Claire Wallace (1992), however, argue that some of Thatcher's policies allowed or even encouraged people to live outside the traditional nuclear family. For example, divorce laws made it relatively easy for married couples to break up, welfare payments made it easier for mothers to be single parents and illegitimate children were given the same rights as those born to married couples.

Abbott and Wallace believe that Margaret Thatcher's government only introduced a limited range of policies to support nuclear families, and the main emphasis was on saving money.

Examiners' notes

New Right perspectives have similarities to the functionalist view of the family but put more emphasis on free-market economics.

Essential notes

This highly conservative view of families, which sought to prevent changes in family life, contrasted with the radical policies of Margaret Thatcher's government which changed many other aspects of the society and economy.

Essential notes

More details on family policies can be found on p 24.

The decline of the nuclear family?

Some New Right thinkers such as Patricia Morgan (2003) think there is strong evidence of a decline in the traditional nuclear family since the 1970s.

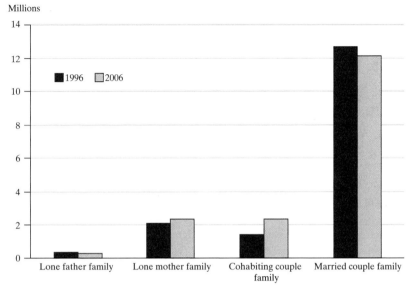

Fig 2
Changes in family types in the UK between 1996 and 2006

Essential notes

Although most of the statistics used by Morgan are accepted, the interpretation of them is not. The changes she describes can be seen as evidence of increasing diversity in families rather than a decline in stability or in the acceptance of family values (see p 36).

Criticisms of the New Right perspective

- Advocates of **family diversity** such as the Rapoports (1989) see increasing diversity as a good thing because it gives people greater freedom to live in the household/family type that best suits them.
- Some sociologists believe that New Right thinkers exaggerate the extent to which family life has changed (see p 36).
- **Feminists** believe that the increase in divorce and single parenthood can be beneficial for women escaping violent, abusive or exploitative relationships with men.
- **Postmodernists** see the declining dominance of nuclear families as part of wider changes in society that are unlikely to be halted by changes in government policies and are in some ways desirable.

Examiners' notes

The critique of this perspective can be developed further by contrasting it with the views of other perspectives.

The family and social change
The relationship between the family and social change
Some theories of the family emphasize the largely unchanging role of the family in society. For example:

- Murdock (see p 4) believed that the family has universal functions and that the nuclear family is typical of all societies.
- **Radical feminists** tend to see families as essentially similar as they are all patriarchal.

Neither of the above approaches acknowledges change in families over time. However, some theorists do acknowledge these changes, including:

- **Liberal feminists** (p 14) believe that the family is getting less patriarchal.
- **Postmodernists** (p 22) believe that families are changing as we move into a postmodern era.

Most of these theories tend to believe that a change in society will lead to a change in the family. Parsons (p 6) believed that a change in the structure of society (from **pre-industrial society** to industrial society) led to a change in the family (from **extended** to **nuclear**). This is illustrated below.

Essential notes

Parsons' concept of structural differentiation looked at on p 7 illustrates how a change in society can lead to a change in the family.

Example: Industrial revolution changes family from extended to nuclear

Change in the social structure

Change in family structure

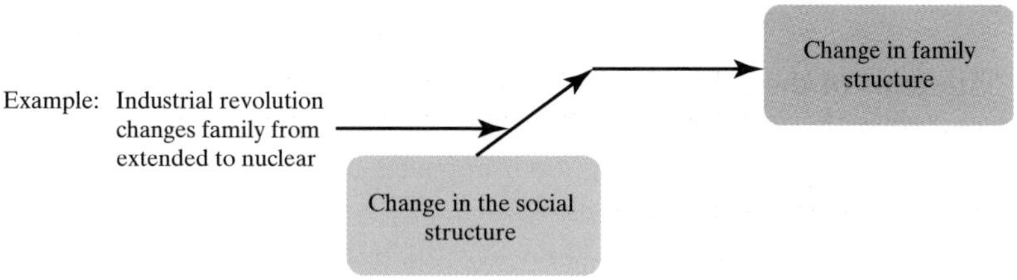

Fig 3
Change from extended to nuclear family

An alternative view is that the family itself can be a cause of change. The structure of the family can shape the direction of change in society. For example, Peter Laslett believed that the dominance of nuclear families helped to cause the Industrial Revolution in some countries.

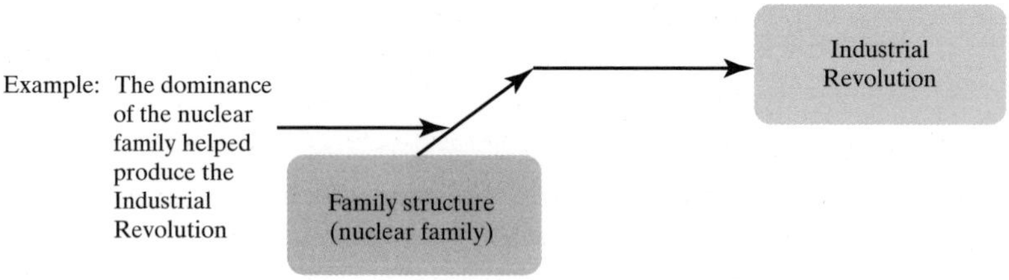

Example: The dominance of the nuclear family helped produce the Industrial Revolution

Family structure (nuclear family)

Industrial Revolution

Fig 4
Dominance of the nuclear family

Key study

Talcott Parsons: the family and industrialization

Talcott Parsons believed that the extended family was well-suited to pre-industrial societies because:

- Most people worked in agriculture. All family members worked the land.

- Many children stayed on the family land.

Therefore large families tended to live together across generations.

However, with the development of industrialization from the 18th century onwards, extended families were no longer well-suited to the social structure. Industrial employment required a **geographically mobile** workforce who could move to new factories, and this was difficult if there were strong ties of dependency with family members such as grandparents and siblings. Extended families also created status problems (see p 7). The development of industrialism therefore led to a decline in the extended family and its replacement with the nuclear family.

Problems with Parsons' theory
- Parsons simply assumed the extended family was the most common family type before the Industrial Revolution.
- Research by Peter Laslett (1972, 1977) found that from 1564 to 1821 only about 10% of households in England contained **kin** beyond the nuclear family.
- Research by Michael Anderson (1971, 1977) focusing on the industrial town of Preston in the mid-19th century found that nearly a quarter of households contained kin other than the nuclear family.
- Research by Michael Young and Peter Wilmot (1973) found that the extended family survived in working-class areas of London into the 1950s.

Laslett – an alternative theory
Peter Laslett found that the nuclear family was the norm in north-west parts of Europe before the Industrial Revolution. He argues that family structure was a factor helping to produce the Industrial Revolution rather than being a consequence of it. **Industrialization** occurred first in Europe because the nuclear family provided the mobile workforce necessary for industry to develop.

The family and social change: conclusion
Although there may be occasions when the structure of the family helps to shape wider changes in society, most sociologists tend to believe that it is changes in society that produce changes in the family. For example:

- The increasing employment of married women outside the home has led to some changes in **conjugal roles** (see p 48).
- Migration and the growth of ethnic minority populations in Britain may have affected the structure of British families (see p 64).

It can be concluded that social structure and family structure are interrelated and affect one another.

Essential notes

Some aspects of Willmott and Young's study have been criticized. For example, feminists such as Oakley have questioned the idea of the symmetrical family, pointing out that Willmott and Young found that many men made only a token contribution to housework.

Essential notes

The middle class might see kin less often than the working class, but the contacts can still be important. For example, middle-class parents might be able to offer more financial support than working-class parents.

Changing family structures

The stages of family development

The development of family structures in Britain has been described in a study by Willmott and Young.

> **Key study**
>
> Willmott and Young (1973) claim that the family has been through three stages.
>
> *Stage 1*: The **pre-industrial** family is a unit of production with parents and children forming the core.
>
> *Stage 2*: The early industrial family extended its network to include other kin. There was a strong bond between married daughters and their mothers who often lived close together, even if not under the same roof. This family type continued into the 1950s in working-class areas such as Bethnal Green in London.
>
> *Stage 3*: In the 1970s the nuclear family became dominant. It was based on a strong **conjugal** bond between husband and wife, and other relatives outside the nuclear family lost importance. Willmott and Young describe this family as **symmetrical**. By this they mean that the husband and wife have similar roles, both do paid work and both do housework and childcare. It developed because of:
>
> - rising wages and a developing **welfare state** making nuclear families more self-reliant
> - increasing **geographical mobility** affecting **kinship networks**
> - improved entertainment and facilities in the home
> - small family size i.e. fewer children per couple.

Families in the 1980s and 1990s

Willmott and Young's research suggests that the extended family will become less and less important as time goes on, but some research contradicts this.

McGlone et al. (1996) argue that **kin** outside the nuclear family are important because they can provide both practical and emotional support. For example, the parents of married children might offer:

- advice
- financial help
- assistance with childcare
- emotional support in times of crisis.

Although kin may live some distance apart, rising living standards, growing car ownership and technological developments make it much easier to keep in touch and to visit one another. McGlone et al. found that contacts remained frequent, with the **working class** having more contact with kin than the **middle class**.

Research findings on the importance of family life

Research suggests that most people continue to attach a great deal of importance to family life, are family centred and do maintain frequent contact.

- McGlone et al. found that most parents believed they should continue to support their children even after they had left home.
- Data from the British Social Attitudes Survey (2001) found that only about 10% of adults did not see their parents frequently and over 60% of grandparents saw their grandchildren at least once a week.
- The British Social Attitudes Survey (2005) shows that the majority of both men (57%) and women (65%) see family members or other relatives weekly or nearly every week. Relatives and friends are about equally important in terms of social contacts, with work colleagues and other acquaintances being much less important. Only a small percentage of men (5%) and women (2%) very rarely or never see other family members.

Family structures in contemporary society

A variety of descriptions have been used to characterize family structures in contemporary Britain.

- Peter Willmott (1988) sees the **dispersed extended family** as typical. Most people live in **nuclear families** but contacts with extended family members who may live some distance apart remain important.
- Julia Brannen (2003) uses the term **beanpole family** to describe families today. She believes there are strong **intergenerational** links between grandparents, children and grandchildren but links with siblings and cousins (**intragenerational** links) are much less important.
- Margaret O'Brien and Deborah Jones (1996) found in research in East London that no one family type is now dominant. Instead there is a **pluralization of lifestyles**. It is therefore pointless to try and find a single family type because family diversity is now the norm (see p 28).

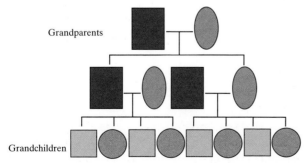

Grandparents

Grandchildren

Essential notes

O'Brien and Jones found the strongest and most conventional family structures amongst the Bangladeshi community.

Essential notes

Theories of diversity contradict the claim that a single family type is dominant.

Fig 5
Beanpole family structure

Essential notes

There is no real debate about the transition taking place between pre-modern/pre-industrial societies and modern industrial societies, but it is disputed whether we have entered an era of post-modernism or not.

The family and modernity

Modernity

Some sociologists divide the development of society into historical time periods. They believe, for example, that society has passed through three stages:

1. pre-modern, **pre-industrial** society
2. **modern,** industrial society
3. **postmodern, post-industrial** society.

In pre-industrial societies, life was relatively stable and predictable, people acted on the basis of tradition, and roles within society were relatively fixed.

The key change with the development of **modernity** (modern society) is that social life becomes based upon **rationality** rather than tradition and the teachings of religion. That is, instead of acting in ways that religious leaders tell them to, or in the ways they have been brought up to behave, people calculate how they should act to achieve certain goals and this guides their behaviour. As a result, social life is less predictable and increased uncertainty and more rapid change is introduced.

The **postmodern era** (see p 22) leads to a decline in rationality. More choices are open to individuals and their **identity** becomes less fixed. This results in even more of the uncertainty and change that was typical of the modern era.

Some of the main changes that have been associated with these eras are summarized in the table below.

Essential notes

This table is only a rough outline of some general views about these changes. More specific details are provided on p 18.

	Pre-modern	Modern	Postmodern
Basis of economy	Agriculture	Industry	Services/ knowledge economy
Social classes	Landowners/ serfs	Bourgeoisie/ proletariat	Classes lose significance
Main belief system	Religion/ tradition	Science/ rationality	No dominant belief system
Main source of identity	Family	Social class	Diverse and image/ lifestyle based. Ethnicity, sexuality become more important
Geographical basis of social life	Local	National	Global
Family life	Based upon established roles and tradition with marriage as the cornerstone	Marriage remains important and the nuclear family is central, but increasing instability develops	Greater choice and variety develops in sexuality and in families and households

Table 4
Stages in the development of Western societies

Other sociologists do not believe that we have yet entered a postmodern era and believe that we still live in modern societies. Their views are examined in this section. According to these sociologists, families have changed as a result of the changes taking place in the modern era (modernity).

Anthony Giddens – relationships in the modern world

Giddens (1992) believes that intimate relationships have changed with modernity.

- In the early period of modernity in the 18th century, marriage became more than an economic arrangement as the idea of romantic love developed. The marriage partner was idealized as someone who would perfect a person's life. Women kept their virginity waiting for the perfect partner.
- In more recent phases of modernity (Giddens calls this **late modernity**), **plastic sexuality** has developed. This means that sex can be for pleasure rather than conceiving children with your perfect marriage partner. Relationships and marriages are no longer seen as necessarily being permanent.
- Marriage is now based on **confluent love** – love that is dependent upon partners benefiting from the relationship. If they are not fulfilled in their relationship, couples no longer stay together out of a sense of duty, so **divorce** and relationship breakdown become more common.

People in late modernity are involved in a **reflexive project of self** – they constantly think about ways of improving their own life. Tradition and societal **norms** no longer tie couples together as they once did.

Beck and Beck-Gernsheim – individualization

Beck and Beck-Gernsheim (1995) see **individualization** as the main characteristic of modern life. This involves:

- More opportunities for individuals, especially women, and the opportunity for individuals to take more and more decisions about every aspect of their lives.
- Little security or intimacy in the everyday world of work, so people seek emotional security in families.
- No generally accepted formula or recipe about love, relationships or family life, so people have to work out their own solutions. For example, the expectations of the roles of husband and wife are no longer clear-cut.
- Conflict resulting from increased choice and uncertainty and also from the pressures of work, where both men and women are expected to compete to achieve career success.
- Increased uncertainty which leads to chaotic personal relationships and helps to explain high **divorce rates**.

Essential notes

The idea of late modernity indicates that Giddens believes we have not yet reached a postmodern era but rather that changes have taken place in modernity.

Essential notes

Beck sees these changes as part of the development of 'risk society' in which people increasingly face risk and uncertainty from man-made problems rather than from hazards in the natural world.

Postmodernity and the family

The main features of **postmodern** society are as follows:

- A rejection of any grand theory which tells people how to live their lives. The postmodernist Jean–François Lyotard (1984) calls this an 'incredulity towards **metanarratives**' – by which he means a lack of faith in any 'big stories' about how society should be run or how people should live. This includes a lack of belief in political ideologies such as Marxism and even a lack of belief in traditional views on marriage and family life.
- Because of this there is increasing **diversity**, choice and fragmentation in social life. People have the ability to choose from a vast array of **identities** and lifestyles and do not have to conform to the way previous generations lived.
- Divisions based on social class or traditional **gender roles** become less important while lifestyle choices become much more important.
- The media and the images presented in the media become more influential in a **media-saturated society**.
- Society changes rapidly as new technology is introduced and improved communications lead to a globalization of social life.

Judith Stacey – the postmodern family

The American sociologist Judith Stacey (1996) believes that the postmodern family has developed in the USA. Based on a study of families in Silicon Valley, California, she describes the postmodern family as 'contested, ambivalent, and undecided'. Stacey believes that in the **modern** era the heterosexual **nuclear family** was judged to be the norm and the closer a family was to that norm the more it was valued. In the postmodern era she sees families as 'diverse, fluid and unresolved'. In other words they:

- are very varied in the structure and form they take
- are constantly changing
- have no set structure that is regarded as the ideal.

For example, gay and lesbian families have to work out their own set of relationships since they cannot model themselves on the heterosexual nuclear family.

Essential notes

Marxists are hostile to postmodernism because they believe that class is still very important in society.

Examiners' notes

These ideas link to the belief that there is increasing family diversity, so can be used in questions on this topic.

Key study

Stacey's ideas are based upon her study of families in Silicon Valley in California, which she sees as a typical **post-industrial** and **postmodern** region specializing in the production of silicon chips.

Stacey uses the example of two families/**kinship networks** to illustrate the nature of postmodern families.

Pam and Dotty

Pam and Dotty were married manual workers at the end of the 1950s and both their husbands worked their way up until they had **middle-class** levels of income. Pam and Dotty did some unskilled manual work

Essential notes

This case study lacks the large sample necessary to be able to make generalizations. Silicon Valley may not be typical of other areas in the USA, never mind the UK.

to boost family income. Pam and Dotty met in the 1970s when they started courses at a local college where they were exposed to feminist ideas. Both were unhappy with the lack of contribution their husbands made to family life and Dotty was physically abused by her husband.

Pam got divorced and started a degree, later marrying a man with whom she had a more equal relationship. She also befriended her first husband's live-in lover to form an unusual **extended kinship network**.

Dotty split up with her husband as well, but eventually took him back after he had had a serious heart attack and was no longer physically able to abuse her. Her husband now had to do most of the housework and Dotty started campaigning for the rights of battered women. After her husband and two of her adult children died, Dotty formed a new household consisting of her, one of her surviving daughters who was a single mother, and four grandchildren.

Pam and Dotty's families demonstrate the fluid and constantly changing family and household structures in Silicon Valley that are typical of postmodernity.

Essential notes

Whatever the limitations of this particular study, there is no doubt that family life is becoming more varied.

Evaluation of postmodern theories of the family

Stacey's study can be criticized for:

- research based on a very small sample of families
- exaggerating the degree of fluidity and uncertainty in family life by picking untypical examples
- underestimating the continuing appeal of heterosexual nuclear families.

However, postmodernism does provide explanations for the increasing **diversity** of family types discussed on p 28.

Social policy and the family

Introduction

The family has sometimes been regarded as a private sphere in which the state should not interfere. However, there is no doubt that in Britain a number of state policies have a direct and indirect impact upon family and that the government sometimes deliberately tries to intervene in aspects of family life. For example, the state can affect family life through:

- Education policies such as the provision of nursery education and compulsory schooling.
- Taxation policies such as the way the incomes of husbands and wives are taxed.
- Legal changes such as changes in divorce law or child protection legislation.
- Housing policy such as the suitability and location of social housing.
- Health and welfare policies, such as 'care in the community', which affects the responsibility of families for relatives.

Country	Policy	Outcome of policy
Communist Soviet Union	The state tried to undermine the family in line with the Marxist view that families would not be necessary in communist societies as they only existed to bolster the power of the ruling class in capitalism. In the 1920s legislation encouraged equality between the sexes and liberalized divorce and abortion laws.	By the 1930s the state was encouraging family life and the role of women in giving birth in order to increase the size of the population.
Kibbutz in Israel	In kibbutzim, children were raised separately from their parents with full-time carers looking after them. Parents lived close by and visited them daily.	Policy was gradually abandoned as conventional family units were preferred by most people.
Communist China	Since 1980, couples who have more than one child have been fined and some parents have been fired from their jobs. Many women have been forced into having abortions. In the countryside parents are allowed to have a second child if the first is a girl but this is not allowed in the cities.	Policy has resulted in a rapidly ageing population and disproportionate number of males (as female foetuses are more likely to be aborted), but has yet to be lifted.

Table 5
Family policies in different societies

Sociological and political perspectives on the family

The New Right

As discussed on p 14, the **New Right** are strongly in favour of conventional **nuclear families** with married heterosexual couples living with their children. They see this family structure as providing stability as well as being independent and self-reliant. If family members care for each other (for example, families taking care of elderly relatives), this reduces state expenditure and allows taxes to be kept low which benefits private enterprise. They also believe that nuclear families pass on a work ethic to their children and this benefits free-market economies.

Charles Murray (1984) argues that an **underclass** has been created through over-generous welfare payments, especially to single parents. Single parenthood is harmful to society because it encourages irresponsible behaviour amongst children who copy the parents. Sons of single mothers miss an adult male role model of a hard-working and responsible father taking care of his family. Daughters of single mothers may follow in the mother's footsteps by having children outside of stable relationships, often while they are young, and then relying upon state benefits to support them.

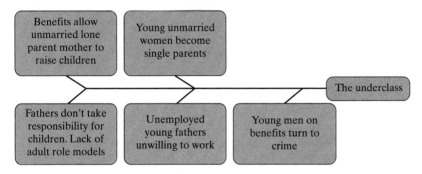

Fig 6
The causes of the underclass

The New Right influenced the policies of Conservative governments between 1979 and 1997, particularly in the period when Margaret Thatcher was in power.

Feminist views

As discussed on p 10, feminists are critical of the **nuclear family**, arguing that it is usually **patriarchal** and biased in favour of men. Feminists believe that social policies generally act to maintain the power of men in families and do little to control men who are violent or abusive to their partners or children. Feminists therefore tend to favour policies which give more choice to women, including liberal divorce laws and tax and benefits policies which make women independent of their male partners.

Examiners' notes

It is useful to refer to different types of gender regime to add theoretical substance to the content of answers.

Key study

An example of feminist research on social policy and family is provided by Eileen Drew (1995), who argues that the policies of different governments follow different **gender regimes** – sets of policies which make different assumptions about family life. There are two main types of gender regime:

- **Familistic gender regimes** favour and support traditional nuclear families in which husbands are expected to be the main breadwinner while wives are expected to concentrate on domestic responsibilities.

- **Individualistic gender regimes** have more egalitarian policies, believing that assumptions should not be made about the roles of husbands and wives and they should be treated equally. This type of gender regime is more tolerant of the choices that individuals make and is more accepting of diversity in family life.

Drew argues that many countries are moving towards a more individualistic gender regime. Whether this is the case in Britain is examined below.

Policies that support conventional families

A number of policies that support conventional families (or familistic gender regimes) have been identified by sociologists. These include:

- The assumption that child benefit should be paid to mothers.
- School hours that assume one parent will be at home in the afternoon making it difficult for **dual-earner families**.
- Limited state provision of care for the elderly and the encouragement of relatives (usually daughters) to provide care.
- According to Fox Harding (1996), housing policies that assume nuclear families should get priority over lone parent families.
- Child support policies that have emphasized the importance of absent parents (usually fathers) paying for their offspring.

Policies that do not support conventional families

Some state policies in Britain have not supported conventional nuclear families and instead appear to favour individualistic gender regimes, e.g:

- The gradual liberalization of **divorce** laws (see p 42).
- The recognition of gay and lesbian relationships.
- Increased provision of state funding for childcare for children under school age (the New Labour government provided 2 ½ hours of childcare per weekday for all three-and four-year-olds).
- Increased police action and concern about domestic violence, particularly that committed by men against women.

Social policies and the family

Supporting conventional families	Undermining conventional families
• Education hours	• Benefits for lone parents
• Child benefit	• Legalization of civil partnerships for gay/lesbian couples
• Family tax credit	
• Family-sized social housing	• Liberal divorce law
• Child support policies for fathers	• State help with childcare for under-fives
• Expectation of family care for elderly	• Prosecution of violent husbands

Policies and political parties

Sociologists have examined the extent to which recent British governments have favoured the view that the conventional, single-earner **nuclear family** is the ideal.

Essential notes

The Child Support Agency was set up in 2003 to pursue maintenance payments and was replaced in 2008 by the Child Maintenance and Support Commission. This prevents single-parent families having to be self-sufficient, although its principal aim may be to save the state money.

Examiners' notes

Answers should balance evidence which suggests that conventional families are supported by policies with evidence that they are not, before reaching a conclusion about the overall effect.

Essential notes

Whatever the philosophy underlying the policies of different parties, in the end most tend to only intervene directly in family life to a limited extent.

New Right governments, 1979 to 1997

According to Pamela Abbott and Claire Wallace (1992), the governments of Margaret Thatcher and John Major followed some policies supporting traditional families. For example:

- They changed taxation policies so that cohabiting couples could no longer claim more in tax allowances than married couples.

However:

- They did not introduce tax or benefits policies to encourage mothers to stay at home.
- They made divorce easier to obtain in 1984.
- They gave illegitimate children the same rights as those born within marriage.

Abbott and Wallace conclude that in reality the New Right had a more balanced approach to families than their ideology would suggest.

New Labour, 1997 to 2010

The New Labour party followed the New Right in arguing that the traditional family was a desirable institution. However:

- New Labour was more willing to accept that family diversity was the norm and that policies should reflect this.
- They allowed **civil partnerships** for gay and lesbian couples and also allowed these couples the right to be able to apply to adopt children.

This suggests that New Labour adopted a more individualistic gender regime than the previous Conservative government.

Some New Labour policies supported nuclear families:

- They gave employees the right to time off work for family reasons.
- They introduced a Working Families Tax Credit .

Jennifer Somerville (2000) claims that Tony Blair's government idealized family life as a 'working example of mutual interdependence, care and responsibility' and increased expectations about parental responsibility, even though it recognized diversity.

Coalition government from 2010

In 2010 David Cameron became Prime Minister in a coalition government between Conservatives and Liberal Democrats. He promised before the election to introduce tax breaks for married couples, suggesting support for conventional nuclear families. However, at the party conference in 2010, it was announced that Child Benefit would be stopped for families with a higher rate taxpayer.

Conclusion

Once in power all recent governments have had to acknowledge the reality of increasing **family diversity** and none have succeeded in reversing a move away from traditional gender roles in conventional nuclear families.

Essential notes

John Major's government introduced a 'back to basics' campaign extolling the virtues of conventional morality and family life, but it was undermined when the infidelity of some cabinet ministers was exposed.

Essential notes

The Working Families Tax Credit helped with the finances of families.

Essential notes

Stopping Child Benefits for families with a higher rate tax payer disadvantages affluent families with a single earner and a stay-at-home mother – dual-earner families could earn much more than single-earner families without losing the benefit.

The growth of family diversity

What is family diversity?

A good deal of historical research on the family has sought to identify the typical family type in different eras. For example, research has examined whether the **nuclear family** is the typical or dominant type in industrial societies. The idea of **family diversity** suggests that in any one era, no particular type of family is dominant or can be considered the norm.

Some historians such as Michael Anderson (1980) have argued that there has always been diversity in family types, but most sociologists of the family before the 1980s assumed that family diversity was not the norm. More recently some sociologists have continued to argue that a single family type is dominant. For example, Peter Willmott (1988) claims that the **dispersed extended family** is the norm and Julia Brannen (2003) believes that the **beanpole family** is now typical in Britain (see p 19).

The cereal packet image of the family

The idea that a single family type is dominant is also found in the media. According to Ann Oakley (1982), marketing and advertising often tries to sell products to what it sees as a typical family. Oakley believes that the image of the typical family presented, for example, in advertising for breakfast cereals, portrays the conventional family as 'nuclear families composed of legally married couples, voluntarily choosing the parenthood of one or more (but not too many) children'. Leach (1967) calls this the **cereal packet image of the family**.

The portrayal of the cereal packet image of the family has been attacked by the American feminist Barrie Thorne (1992). Thorne believes that gender, generation, race and class result in widely varying experiences of family life, many of which diverge from the nuclear family with the male **breadwinner** and female housewife.

Oakley, Leach and Thorne all see this stereotype of the nuclear family as highly misleading, and the idea that diversity or variation in families is normal has been developed by other sociologists.

Family diversity in Britain

Robert and Rhona Rapoport (1982) were the first British sociologists to point out that nuclear family households have become a minority in Britain. Since they first wrote about diversity, nuclear families have continued to become a smaller proportion of all households in Great Britain.

In table 7 the categories 'One family household with 1–2, or 3 or more dependent children' represent the nuclear family. In 1971 35% of households were of this type but by 2008 the figure had decreased to 21%. The table shows that there have been increases in the percentage of households consisting of one person under or over state pension age, a couple, and lone parents with dependent or non-dependent children.

Examiners' notes

It is useful to discuss diversity when answering any questions about the structure of the family today because diversification is an essential part of all recent trends in family life.

Examiners' notes

Note that the ideas of both Oakley and Thorne can also be used to answer questions about the contribution of feminists to an understanding of the family.

Household types increasing 1971–2008	One person households under pension age.
	One person households over pension age.
	Couple only households.
	Lone parent households with dependent children.
	Lone parent households with non-dependent children.
Household types decreasing 1971–2008	One family households with 1–2 dependent children.
	One family households with three or more dependent children.
	One family households with non-dependent children.
	Households with two or more unrelated adults.

Examiners' notes

To give a rounded answer to questions about family diversity you will also need to look at p 31, which includes some alternative interpretations of the trends shown in these statistics. Not everybody agrees that the figures show a serious decline in nuclear families.

Table 6
Growing and declining household types, 1971–2008

Households: by type of household and family

Great Britain

	1971	1981	1991	2001	2008
One person households					
Under state pension age	6%	8%	11%	14%	15%
Over state pension age	12%	14%	16%	15%	15%
One family households					
Couple					
No children	27%	26%	28%	29%	29%
1–2 dependent children	26%	25%	20%	19%	18%
3 or more dependent children	9%	6%	5%	4%	3%
Non-dependent children only	8%	8%	8%	6%	6%
Lone parent					
Dependent children	3%	5%	6%	7%	7%
Non-dependent children only	4%	4%	4%	3%	3%
Two or more unrelated adults	4%	5%	3%	3%	3%
Multi-family households	1%	1%	1%	1%	1%
All households					
(= 100%)	18.6%	20.2%	22.4%	23.9%	25.0%

Table 7
Data on households in the UK, 1971–2008

These changes represent an increase in the diversity of family structures and in the proportion of households with a structure other than that of the nuclear family.

29

Types of diversity

The Rapoports (1982) identify five main types of diversity:

1. **Organizational diversity**. This involves variations in family structure, household type, kinship network and the **division of labour** within the home. Examples include **lone-parent families**, **dual-earner families**, **cohabiting** couples and **reconstituted families** (families formed out of the fragments of previous families after a divorce). Reconstituted families can include stepchildren, half brothers and sisters and so on.
2. Cultural diversity. This refers to differences in lifestyles between families of different ethnic, national or religious backgrounds; for example, differences between British Asian and white British families, British and Polish families, Catholic and Protestant families.
3. **Class** diversity. There are also differences in families of upper-class, middle-class and working-class origin. These might impact on relationships between adults and the way children are socialized.
4. Stage in the **life-cycle**. For example, there are differences between newly married couples without children, couples with dependent children and families with non-dependent children.
5. Cohort. A cohort is a group of people born over the same period of time (e.g. the baby boomer generation born in the period 1946 to 1964). This generation is sometimes seen as having a different pattern of family life than their parents' generation; for example, having more dual-earner families.

Reasons for diversification

Graham Allan and Graham Crow (2001) believe that diversification has continued. There is no longer a fixed set of stages in the life-cycle and each family follows a more unpredictable course, complicated by cohabitation, **divorce**, remarriage, and so on. This reflects greater individual choice and 'the increasing separation of sex, marriage and parenthood'.

They give the following reasons for increasing diversity:

- A rising **divorce rate** caused by factors such as changes in the divorce law, rising social acceptance of divorce and greater independence for women.
- An increase in lone parent households partly resulting from increasing divorce, also from greater acceptance of births outside marriage.
- Cohabitation has become increasingly acceptable, partly as a result of the decline in the influence of religion (secularization).
- Declining marriage rates, as people marry later and an increasing minority choose not to marry at all.
- The rise in the number of **stepfamilies** as a result of increases in divorce.

Rates of cohabitation have increased, with each cohort adding to family diversity.

The number of people marrying is falling but more than a quarter of marriages are remarriages, leading to the formation of more reconstituted families.

New types of diversity

Over recent decades, new types of **diversity** in addition to those identified by the Rapoports have developed as a result of liberalization in attitudes to sexuality and the introduction of **new reproductive technologies**.

- Weeks, Heaphey and Donovan (1999) see the increase in openly **gay and lesbian households** and families as contributing to the increase in diversity. They believe that gay men and lesbians often see their households and even their friendship networks as being **chosen families**. On the basis of this they argue that an important social change is taking place in which whom we see to be part of our family is more important than ties of blood or marriage. **Friendship networks** can now function as if they were families. This is part of a general move towards a greater emphasis on individual choice rather than the duties and obligations of family life.
- Roseneil (2005) links the development of chosen families to the breakdown of the **heteronorm** – the belief that all intimate relationships should be based on heterosexuality. TV programmes such as *Friends* and *Will and Grace* highlight the possibility that there are alternative networks to traditional families.

New reproductive technologies

New reproductive technologies date from 1978 when the first 'test-tube baby', Louise Brown, was born through in-vitro fertilization.

Surrogate motherhood, where one woman carries a foetus produced by the egg of another woman, is now possible. This raises questions about who the parents of the child are since the birth parents and the genetic parents are different. It adds to the complexity of possible family types and has even led to a grandmother giving birth to her own grandchild.

Essential notes

The Civil Partnerships Act of 2004 in the UK recognized and legitimized gay and lesbian relationships.

Examiners' notes

The idea of chosen families is extremely useful in answering a wide range of questions. It challenges conventional definitions of the family since it means that families are no longer based on kinship or marriage and it can therefore be used to question most of the theories of the family. It does, however, fit with the postmodern view of the family which sees traditional assumptions about the family as no longer being accepted.

Family diversity and lone parenthood

The growth of single parenthood

Lone parenthood can come about through a number of different routes. People who are married can become lone parents through **divorce**, **separation** or the death of a spouse. Similarly, **cohabiting** parents who are not married and have children can split up or one of them die. It can also result from births to women who do not live with the father of the child.

As table 8 shows, in 2007 nearly one in five single women, and more than a third of divorced women who were not cohabiting with a man, lived with a dependent child or children. For married couples the most likely situation was to live with one or more children, but living with parents was common amongst all the non-married groups in the table.

Percentages of women with:	Dependent children	Non-dependent children only	No children
Married	53%	16%	31%
Non-married			
Cohabiting	44%	4%	52%
Single	18%		81%
Widowed	15%	35%	51%
Divorced	37%	23%	41%
Separated	65%	9%	26%
All working-age women (Women aged 16 to 59).	**42%**	**11%**	**47%**

Table 8
Women in the UK with or without children in the household, 2007

Lone parent households have grown rapidly over recent decades, with government statistics for the United Kingdom showing that between 1971 and 2008 the percentage of households consisting of lone parents and dependent children has risen from 3% to 7%.

Demographic causes of lone parenthood

Allan and Crow (2001) explain the increase in lone parenthood in terms of two factors:

- an increase in **marital breakdown** (particularly divorce)
- a rise in births to unmarried mothers.

They suggest that both these trends can be explained in terms of an increasing acceptance of diversity and choice in family life. (See pp 38-39 for explanations of rising divorce).

David Morgan (1994) sees changing relationships between men and women as important, with greater equality between the sexes making it more feasible for women to bring up children on their own. In addition, more employment opportunities for women encourage them to have a life in which they are not dependent upon a male partner.

Changing attitudes and lone parenthood

Evidence from the British Social Attitudes Survey (2001) shows that younger age groups are much more accepting of parenthood outside marriage. It is no longer regarded as necessary to legitimize a birth by having a 'shotgun wedding' before a child is born to an unmarried couple. David Morgan (1994) notes that much less stigma is now attached to **illegitimacy**. However, research by Burghes and Brown (1995) suggests that most lone parents do not regard the situation as ideal and the British Social Attitudes Survey found there is still disapproval of teenage pregnancies.

Dependency culture

According to Charles Murray (1999) the increase in lone parenthood is a result of an over-generous welfare system which makes it possible for lone parents to live on benefits with housing provided by the state. Murray sees lone parents as part of a welfare-dependent **underclass**.

Murray's views have been strongly criticized for being based on limited research.

Allan and Crow (2001) point out that most lone mothers find a new partner within a few years and do not rely on benefits throughout an offspring's childhood. This view is supported by research by the Department for Work and Pensions (2004).

The effects of lone parenthood

Some research suggests that lone parenthood can lead to a range of negative consequences, particularly for the children. These include:

- a greater chance of living in **poverty**
- children doing less well in education
- children being more likely to become delinquent or to use drugs.

However, more sophisticated research suggests that any negative effects are more the result of low income than the lack of two parents, and E.E. Cashmore (1985) points out that having one parent may be better for children than having two parents if the absent parent is abusive or violent.

Examiners' notes

The section on the changing birth rate (pp 58–61) includes some useful material on reasons for births to young mothers, some of whom will not be living with a partner. Be sure to include this material if asked a longer question on the reasons for a rise in lone parenthood.

Examiners' notes

Charles Murray is associated with the theory of the New Right – his ideas are dealt with on p 25. This perspective can be criticized using other theories, particularly feminism and postmodernism. Incorporating criticisms from competing theoretical perspectives helps to get you into the top mark band.

Essential notes

Many studies which claim there are negative effects of lone parenthood for children can be criticized on methodological grounds. Most use small samples and fail to control for the effects of low income on outcomes for children. More sophisticated research does control for the effects of low income/poverty and this tends to find less strong evidence of negative consequences.

Ethnicity and family diversity

Ethnicity and diversity

- **Ethnic groups** are groups within a population regarded by themselves or others as culturally distinctive; they usually see themselves as having a common origin. Ethnicity may be linked to religion, nationality and other aspects of culture such as language and lifestyle.
- Largely as a result of **migration**, Britain has a number of distinctive ethnic groups. The largest minority ethnic groups in Britain are those of South Asian or African Caribbean origin. The Irish and Chinese can also be regarded as minority ethnic groups.
- Minority ethnic groups can be seen as adding to the diversity of family types in Britain to the extent that they have distinctive family patterns or lifestyles. If their family life has become very similar to that of the white British majority then minority ethnic groups may not contribute to the **diversity.**

The extent of ethnic diversity

The 2001 census found significant differences in the family life of ethnic groups in Britain. For example:

- In 2001 8% of white and 7% of Black-Caribbean households were headed by an unmarried **cohabiting** couple compared to just 2% of British Asian households.
- 23% of Black-Caribbean households were **lone parent families** compared to 8% of Indian and 9% of white British households.
- Black-Caribbean **lone parents** are much more likely to be single (71%) than Bangladeshi lone parents (5%).
- In 2001, 71% of Black-Caribbean adults were single (never married) compared to 39% of white British adults, but just 8% of Pakistanis and 5% of Bangladeshis.

	One person house-holds (%)	Pensioner families	Married couple families	Cohabiting couple families	Lone parent families	Other house-holds
White British	31	9	37	8	9	6
Indian	15	3	53	2	8	19
Pakistani	12	1	51	2	11	23
Bangladeshi	9	1	54	2	11	24
Black-Caribbean	38	3	19	7	23	9
Chinese	28	2	41	4	8	16
All households	30	9	37	8	10	7

Table 9
UK households by ethnic group, 2001

Studies of Asian families

Research by Bhatti (1999) using in-depth interviews of Asian families in southern England found a strong emphasis on family loyalty and on trying to maintain traditional family practices. Izzat, the principle of family honour, was taken very seriously and mothers saw their family roles as the most important duty in life. Fathers usually took on the traditional **breadwinner** role. This evidence suggests that Asian families add to diversity by maintaining traditional, nuclear families but with very strong **extended kinship networks** and a strong sense of mutual obligation.

However, there was some evidence that life in Britain has begun to erode the distinctiveness of Asian families, with increasing numbers of clashes between younger and older generations. In some families children rebelled against traditional values, for example by seeking to marry outside their own community against parental wishes.

A study of British Asians living in Brick Lane – the heart of the Bangladeshi community in Britain – by the Policy Studies Institute (1997) found that British South Asians were more likely to marry and to marry earlier than white counterparts and that rates of **divorce** and lone parenthood were low, although they were beginning to increase.

Studies of African Caribbean families

The Policy Studies Institute (1997) found that British African Caribbean households had fewer long-term partnerships than other groups, were more likely to have children outside marriage and had above average rates of divorce and **separation**.

Research by Mary Chamberlain (1999) has found that brothers, sisters, uncles and aunts play a more important role in African Caribbean families than in white British families. Siblings often play a significant part in bringing up younger brothers and sisters and women are quite likely to assist sisters in bringing up children.

Tracey Reynolds (2002) argues that despite the large number of female-headed households amongst Black-Caribbean families in Britain, in reality diversity is the main characteristic of family life in this group. As well as conventional **nuclear families** and **female-headed families**, **visiting relationships** are also common where the female head of household has a male partner who visits them frequently but does not live under the same roof.

Conclusion

The evidence suggests that ethnic minorities do continue to add to the diversity of family life, though there has been a limited degree of convergence with the family life of white British families.

Examiners' notes

You can get into a higher mark band by showing that you are aware of differences between specific ethnic groups. For example, amongst South Asians there are significant differences, with considerably higher rates of one person households amongst Indians (15%) than Bangladeshis (9%).

Examiners' notes

Markers will be looking to see if you have compared patterns of family life in ethnic minorities with majority, white British, patterns and if you have demonstrated an awareness of changes over time. Use the studies to indicate whether the family life of different ethnic groups is becoming more similar over time.

Essential notes

Some sociologists have claimed that there is a distinctive family type among the black population of the Caribbean and the Americas dominated by mothers who are lone parents but get support from other female relatives. Chamberlain's study provides some evidence that this family type has been imported to Britain.

Diversity and the decline of conventional families

The implications of family diversity

Some researchers see increasing **diversity** as not only part of a decline of the **nuclear family** but also as undermining this institution as a model of a conventional family. The following key study backs up this view.

Examiners' notes

This is a very useful study which can be used to answer questions on a wide range of topics including: changes in family structure, ethnicity and diversity, modernity and postmodernity and the family, as well as family diversity. You will be rewarded for quoting specific studies to back up or to criticize theories.

Key study

Dench, Gavron and Young (2006) carried out a study in Bethnal Green in the 1990s to follow up Young and Willmott's study of the area from the 1950s (see p 18). They found that earlier family patterns where working-class residents lived in nuclear families with strong kinship links had largely disappeared. They have been replaced by a new **individualism** in which **cohabitation**, **divorce**, **separation** and **lone parenthood** were all more common. Only the local Bangladeshi population had a dominant pattern of conventional family life based upon marriage and the male **breadwinner**.

Such research has led commentators such as Brenda Almond (2006) to claim that the family is fragmenting (breaking into pieces) and is more concerned with the needs of adult members than creating a stable unit in which children can be raised.

Robert Chester – the neo-conventional family

The widespread view that the nuclear family is threatened by diversity and is breaking up or even disappearing has been challenged by Robert Chester (1985). He found that the following main features of family life have remained fairly stable since the Second World War:

- Most people still get married.
- Most children are reared by their natural parents.
- Most people live in a household headed by a married couple.
- Most people stay married.

Although the situation has changed since Chester was writing, most of the above is still true. (Although the proportion of marriages ending in divorce is now approaching 50%.)

Examiners' notes

Chester's views can be used to balance the ideas of those who believe in increasing diversity, including postmodernists. You are more likely to get into the top mark bands for the essay style questions if you can evaluate competing viewpoints.

Chester argues that the statistics used to support the idea of increasing diversity can be misleading. They are usually based upon the proportion of households of different types and not the proportion of people living in different types of household. This makes a significant difference because nuclear family households tend to be larger than other households since by definition they contain at least two adults and one child. Table 10 shows the percentage of the adult population living in different household types.

Great Britain					
	1971	1981	1991	2001	2008
One person households	6%	8%	11%	12%	12%
One family households					
Couple:					
No children	19%	20%	23%	25%	25%
Dependent children	52%	47%	41%	38%	36%
Non-dependent children only	10%	10%	11%	9%	9%
Lone parent	4%	6%	10%	11%	11%
Other households	9%	9%	4%	5%	6%
All people in private households	53.4%	53.9%	54.1%	56.7%	58.8%

Table 10
Adults in UK households: by type of household and family

The table shows that in 2008, 70% of people were still living in households headed by a couple. This represented a fall from 81% in 1971 but was still a large majority of the population.

Not all of these families were nuclear families in the sense of including both parents and dependent children but, as Chester points out, couples without dependent children often go on to have children later. Furthermore some one-person households consist of widows and widowers who were once married but whose children have now grown up. Chester concludes that most people still live in nuclear families for much of their lives.

Chester believes that one major change has taken place in the life of nuclear families, a change in the roles of husband and wife. He accepts that, increasingly, married women are employed outside the home and he calls this type of family, in which both parents have paid employment, the **neo-conventional family**.

Conclusion

Elizabeth Silva and Carol Smart (1999) agree with Chester that cohabiting or married couples, many of whom have children or go on to have children, remain very important in contemporary family life.

Jennifer Somerville (2000) agrees the decline in traditional families can be exaggerated but also emphasizes that there are important changes taking place. These include:

- Sex outside marriage becoming common.
- More couples who choose not to have children.
- Increasing numbers of lone parents.
- Greater diversity as a result of variations in the family life of different **ethnic groups**.

Essential notes

These views offer some support to those who have tried to identify a single dominant family type in Britain today, such as Julia Brannen, who used the concept of the beanpole family (see p 19). Silva, Smart and Somerville recognize the existence of diversity more than Brannen.

Changing patterns of marriage and cohabitation

Marriage under threat

Some commentators such as Patricia Morgan (2003) believe that the institution of marriage is under threat from a range of factors. These include:

- Falling marriage rates and people marrying at a later age,
- The growth and increasing acceptance of alternatives to marriage including **cohabitation** and staying single.
- An increase in **single-person households.**
- Declining **fertility** and **birth rates** even to those who are married.
- Rising **divorce rates** (examined on pp 40–43).

Marriage rates

Fig 7 shows trends in first marriage in England and Wales since 1862 and shows that despite a rising population the number of marriages has decreased considerably since the 1940s. In 2006 there were 237,000 marriages in England and Wales, which was the lowest recorded number since 1895.

Essential notes

The marriage rate is the number of people per 1000 of the single population getting married each year.

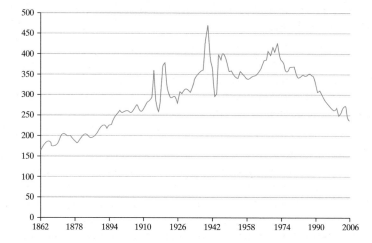

Fig 7
Trends in first marriage in England and Wales since 1862

Examiners' notes

You can use data on the changes in marriage rates to answer questions which ask you to discuss whether the family is in decline. Try to remember some simple statistics which will give you solid support for the points you make.

Between 1995 and 2005, marriage rates fell from just under 35 males marrying per 1000 unmarried males to under 25 per 1000. One reason for the decline in marriage rates may be a delay in the timing of marriage, with both men and women tending to delay their first marriage until later in life. Between 1996 and 2006, age at first marriage rose from 29.3 to 31.8 years for men, and for women from 27.2 to 29.7 years.

However, since first marriage rates are declining in all age groups it is not just a question of delaying marriage; each successive generation is less likely to get married. Research by Ben Wilson and Steve Smallwood (2007) shows that rates of marriage in England and Wales have fallen for the cohorts of women born in each year between 1974 and 1986.

Explanations for declining marriage rates

Declining marriage rates may be caused by several factors which have made marriage less popular. These include:

- Changing social attitudes which see marriage as less socially desirable than in the past and living outside marriage as more acceptable.
- A decline in religious belief (**secularization**) which weakens commitment to marriage as an institution.
- An increase in cohabitation (see below).
- A greater emphasis on **individualism** (see p 21 and p 26).

However, declining marriage does not necessarily indicate a decline in commitment to long-term relationships; for example:

- Civil partnerships among gay and lesbian couples have increased.
- Wilson and Smallwood (2007) point out that marriage rates do not include people married abroad and there is an increasing trend for British couples to travel outside the country to marry.

Cohabitation

Cohabitation has increased rapidly. According to the General Household Survey, in 1979 in Great Britain less than 3% of females were cohabiting but by 2005 this had risen to more than 12%.

In 2004/5, 29% of cohabiting women were divorced, 27% single, 23% separated and 6% widowed.

Patricia Morgan (2003) sees rising cohabitation as part of a trend in which marriage is going out of fashion. Rather than being a prelude to marriage, Morgan believes that it represents an increase in the number of sexual partners and the frequency of partner change. She notes that cohabiting couples tend to stay together for a shorter time than married couples.

Joan Chandler (1993) disagrees, seeing cohabitation as a relatively stable, long-term alternative to marriage.

The British Social Attitudes Survey (2001) has found evidence of increasing acceptance of cohabitation outside marriage, with younger age groups being more likely to find it acceptable than older age groups. However, these surveys have found that there continues to be strong support for long-term, heterosexual relationships. On average, cohabitants in the survey had lived together for 6½ years.

Examiners' notes

To get in the top mark band for essay questions, answers may well require some theoretical content, so make reference to theories of modernity and postmodernity if appropriate.

Examiners' notes

You can always get extra marks for making methodological points, and this point raised by Wilson and Smallwood can be used to question the validity of statistics on marriage rates.

Essential notes

Morgan supports New Right theories (see p 14) so she argues that these changes are part of a pattern of moral decline. She would prefer to see a return to longer relationships, preferably within marriage. Supporters of diversity, though, see these changes as a welcome increase in individual choice.

Divorce and marital breakdown

Types of marital breakdown

Marital breakdown involves the failure or ending of a marriage. This can be divided into three main categories:

1. **Divorce**, the legal ending of a marriage.
2. **Separation**, the physical separation of spouses so that they live apart.
3. **'Empty-shell marriages'**, in which husbands and wives continue to live together and remain legally married, but their relationship has broken down.

Trends in divorce

Long-term, the **divorce rate** (the number of people divorcing per thousand of the married population) has risen dramatically. In 1911 there were just 859 petitions for divorce in England and Wales but in 2008 there were more than 143,000 divorces.

More recently there has been some decline in divorce, with the rate in 2008 the lowest since 1979.

Examiners' notes

If you are asked to define the divorce rate for a 2-mark question you must use the exact definition given here to get both marks. If you aren't sure of the definition of a rate, it is worth remembering that rates in this topic are usually defined as per thousand per year **of the relevant group**.

Fig 8
Divorces in England and Wales
1971–2008

Patterns of divorce

The Office for National Statistics figures for England and Wales show that in 2008:

- The mean (average) age of divorce for men was 43 and for women 41.
- The **median** duration of marriage was 11.5 years.
- In nearly a third of marriages at least one partner had been previously widowed or divorced.
- 28% of men divorcing and 20% of women divorcing had been married and divorced previously.
- 67% of divorce decrees were awarded to women and 33% to men.
- 50% of couples divorcing have at least one child under 16.

Examiners' notes

The high proportion of divorces initiated by women is sometimes used as evidence by feminists to support the view that women are disadvantaged and exploited within marriage. However, when answering a question on feminism you can also make the point that it has become easier for women to escape unsatisfactory marriages.

Separation statistics

There are no reliable figures for separation. However, the 2001 census found that around 2% of adults are separated and living alone in Britain.

Judicial separations increased rapidly in the 1960s but as no figures are produced for unofficial separations, it is impossible to say whether this represented a real increase in total separations or not. Judicial separations are now uncommon because divorce is easier to obtain and both partners are more likely to accept divorce than in the past.

Empty-shell marriages

There are no reliable estimates of the number of **empty-shell marriages**. This is partly because it is very difficult to define empty-shell marriages and to operationalize any definition when conducting research.

However, impressionistic historical evidence does suggest that in the past people were more likely to accept an unsatisfactory marriage than today because divorce was almost impossible to obtain. For example, William Goode (1971) argues that empty-shell marriages were common in 19th-century America, when couples tended to stay together for the sake of their children and to preserve their social standing in the community.

Explanations for marital breakdown

Nicky Hart (1976) points out that explaining marital breakdown can involve three types of factor:

- Factors affecting the value attached to marriage.
- Factors affecting the degree of conflict between spouses.
- Factors affecting opportunities to escape from marriage.

The value of marriage

The **functionalist** Ronald Fletcher (1966) believed divorce has increased because people attach more value to marriage than in the past. If marriage is so important to individuals, they are more likely to seek divorce if their marriage is unsatisfactory. However, the British Social Attitudes Survey (2007) found that people do continue to value marriage but there is no evidence that the value attached has been increasing. Furthermore, cohabitation is increasingly accepted as an alternative to marriage.

Conflict between spouses

A number of possible reasons for increasing conflict between spouses have been put forward.

- Functionalists such as Goode (1971) believe that conflict has increased because the **nuclear family** is becoming more isolated from other **kin**, placing an emotional burden on husbands and wives who have little support from other relatives.
- According to Dennis (1975), because the nuclear family specializes in fewer **functions**, the bonds between husband and wife are the main force holding the family together. Therefore if love goes there is little to prevent marital breakdown.
- Allan and Crowe (2001) believe marital breakdown has increased because the family is less likely to be an economic unit (for example running a family firm), making it easier for spouses to split up.

Essential notes

Operationalizing means the measurement of abstract concepts by defining them in research, for example by writing questionnaire questions. Divorce is easy to measure because it is defined legally, but separation and empty-shell marriages are harder to define and operationalize.

Examiners' notes

The problems of defining the different types of marital breakdown can be used to make the point that the validity of all of the statistics for measuring total marital breakdowns is open to question.

Examiners' notes

To get into the top mark band make some links between these points and functionalist theory in general.

Examiners' notes

You can develop Gibson's point further by linking it to the ideas of Beck and Giddens, whose theories suggest a similar relationship between modernity and changes in personal relationships (see p 21).

Modernity, freedom and choice

Colin Gibson (1994) links increased marital breakdown to **modernity**. He argues that individual competition and a free-market economy have placed increased emphasis on **individualism**. Individuals pursue personal satisfaction and are accustomed to the idea of consumer choice and fulfilment coming from such choice. Marriage is therefore treated like other consumer products and if it is not providing satisfaction it is more likely to be discarded.

The ease of divorce

Changing social attitudes have made it easier for people to contemplate divorce.

- Divorce has become more socially acceptable. The British and European Social Attitudes Survey (1998) found that 82% of people in Britain disagreed that married couples should stay together even if they didn't get along.
- Colin Gibson (1994) believes that **secularization** (the decline of religious belief) has loosened the rigid morality which in the past made divorce morally unacceptable to some people.
- Gibson also argues that society lacks shared values which may operate to stabilize marriage.

A wide range of laws have been introduced which make divorce both easier and cheaper to obtain. These laws have undoubtedly affected the divorce rate. For example, the Divorce Reform Act of 1971 removed the idea that one party had to be found guilty of some form of misbehaviour to allow divorce. This was followed by a large increase in divorce as more couples took advantage of the easier process of divorcing. Changing divorce laws are summarized in the table below.

Essential notes

It is important to learn some of the key dates and changes in legislation to give substance to longer answers on marital breakdown and the decline of the family. This will show that you understand that the changing rates of divorce might reflect changing laws as much as changing attitudes to marriage.

Legislation and date	Details of legislation	Consequences of legislation
Law before 1857	Divorce was only available through Acts of Parliament.	Divorce was too expensive for all but the most wealthy families so only a handful of divorces took place.
1857 Matrimonial Causes Act	The idea of matrimonial offence created, with adultery the main grounds for divorce.	Divorce became easier and cheaper to obtain but normally only if adultery could be established.
1950 Divorce Law	Grounds for divorce widened to include cruelty and desertion.	Divorce still based upon blaming one spouse for the breakdown of the marriage.
Divorce Reform Act 1971	Main grounds for divorce was now the 'irretrievable breakdown' of the marriage rather than actions of one spouse.	Made it much easier to obtain divorce without having to demonstrate that one partner had behaved badly.

Divorce Law 1984	Reduced the time before a divorce petition could take place from three years to one. Behaviour of partners to be taken into account in financial awards.	Made it quicker to get a divorce if the marriage was not successful.
Family Law Act 1996	It was no longer necessary to prove irretrievable breakdown, partners simply had to state that it had broken down. A period of reflection was introduced before divorce could be finalized, and greater use of mediation encouraged.	Aimed to increase the stability of marriage but made divorce easier in some ways.

Table 11
Changing divorce law

Divorce has become a more affordable proposition as a result of changes in laws which affect the cost of getting a divorce or provide support for those who have been divorced:

- In 1949 the Legal Aid and Advice Act provided for free advice for those who could not afford to pay a solicitor.
- The Child Support, Pensions and Social Security Act of 2000 laid down fixed contributions that absent parents had to pay for their children, making it easier for parents (usually the mother) to retain some economic security after divorce.

Conclusion

A rising divorce rate is just one of a range of social changes that seem to indicate a decline in the popularity of marriage. Others include a rising number of lone parents and single-person households, and an increase in **cohabitation**.

However, all these changes are open to interpretation, and Robert Chester (1985) says, 'on the evidence, most people will continue not only to spend most of their lives in a family environment, but also to place a high value on it'. Furthermore, high rates of remarriage after divorce suggest that it is particular marriages that many people are rejecting rather than the idea of marriage itself.

Jennifer Somerville (2000) points out that the vast majority of people in Britain still get married, most people live in a household headed by a married couple and **extended kinship networks** remain strong. She therefore concludes that rather than a simple decline in the institution of marriage, there has been a diversification of family forms and relationships.

The changing life course

The life-cycle

The term the **life-cycle** is often used to refer to the experiences of those passing through stages of life. The idea of the life-cycle is illustrated below.

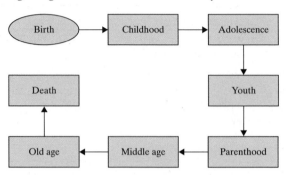

Fig 9
The life-cycle

The idea of the life-cycle implies there are set stages through which people pass.

An example of this approach to define an individual's progress is provided by the **functionalist** Talcott Parsons (1954). He saw people as passing through distinctive age groups with different social roles associated with each age group:

- Childhood, the period when **socialization** into society's culture takes place.
- Adolescence, when children begin to develop independence from their parents so that ultimately they can shift their allegiance from their parents to their marriage partner.
- Old age, which results in the loss of important social roles.

The life course

However, according to Jane Pilcher (1995), in reality there is no universal life-cycle because:

- Not everyone passes through every stage (for example, not everybody becomes a parent).
- Ageing is experienced differently within and between societies.

Pilcher therefore uses the term **life course** instead of life-cycle. She defines life course as 'a socially defined timetable of behaviours deemed appropriate for particular life stages within any one society'.

In different societies the life course will be seen differently; for example, in Western societies youthfulness may be valued more than in tribal societies. Even within a society it can be viewed differently; for example, women may value youthfulness more than men.

The life course is also affected by **life expectancy**. As life expectancy has increased in advanced Western societies, so perceptions of when middle age and old age start have changed.

Essential notes

The idea of the life course can be illustrated by using the material on childhood as a social construct, which is found on pp 52–53. As well as varying between societies, the nature of the life course changes over time as illustrated by changing conceptions of childhood.

Class, gender and the life course

Conflict perspectives such as Marxism and **feminism** emphasize inequality between different age groups, arguing that the life course is affected by wealth, income and access to resources. John Vincent (1995, 2006) believes that different classes and males and females experience ageing differently. For example, older women are more likely to experience life after retirement as a period of poverty and struggle because they generally have less entitlement to occupational pensions than men.

In general, Western capitalist societies attach more importance to age than other societies and being of working age has become increasingly important since this provides access to most people's main source of income – employment.

Age categories as a social construction

The idea of a fixed life-cycle is completely rejected by those who regard age categories as **socially constructed**. From this point of view, biological ageing has little or nothing to do with the expectations associated with different age groups. Society constructs these expectations and in doing so shapes what people believe to be normal behaviour.

Jenny Hockey and Allison James (1993) illustrate this approach in their research on old age. They believe old age is stereotyped in the media, and the elderly are treated as similar to children: old age is infantilized. For example, in old people's homes the elderly are allowed few choices so that they are marginalized, excluded and made dependent.

The **postmodernists** Featherstone and Hepworth (1991) believe that the life course has been **deconstructed** or has broken down. Clear-cut distinctions between age groups have become less and less important. **De-differentiation** has taken place where stages in the life-cycle have become less distinctive. They give the following examples:

- Children and adults have become less distinctive in the way they dress and in their leisure pursuits.
- Exposure to mass media means children are more aware of adult life.
- The middle class spend more on body maintenance to slow down ageing.
- Older people are more healthy and take more part in youthful lifestyles and leisure activities than in the past.

Featherstone and Hepworth conclude that **personal age** – how old people see themselves – is more important than **chronological age**, the number of years they have lived.

Examiners' notes

A useful tip for getting into the top mark band on many questions is to show you understand that there are differences in people's experiences based upon their class, gender, ethnicity and age. Mentioning this allows you to include extra evaluation if a perspective or theory emphasizes one of these differences more than others. (For example, feminists tend to emphasize gender to the exclusion of other social divisions.)

Examiners' notes

Featherstone and Hepworth can be included in any exam answers on postmodern theory, childhood or on questions about the changing relationships within the family.

Conjugal roles, housework and childcare

Types of conjugal role

Conjugal roles are the roles of husband and wife within marriage.

Two main types of conjugal role have been distinguished:

1. Segregated **conjugal roles**. The roles of husband and wife are very different. The husband is the main **breadwinner** and has little involvement with housework and childcare. Husbands tend to spend leisure time away from the family with male friends while women spend more time with female kin such as their mothers and sisters.
2. **Joint conjugal roles** involve men and women doing some paid work and also both spouses being involved with housework and childcare. Typically, with this type of conjugal role, men and women spend more time together and less time with their own groups of same sex friends.

These two types of conjugal role are extremes and often roles will be somewhere in between.

The symmetrical family

Young and Willmott (1973) claimed that joint conjugal roles were becoming more common in the **symmetrical family**. They found a move towards greater equality within marriage in that wives were now going out to work and husbands were providing more help with housework.

These views were heavily criticized by Ann Oakley (1974), who notes that in Young and Willmott's research a family was regarded as symmetrical if the husbands did any housework at least once a week. This hardly represented equality within a household. Her own research found that few men had high levels of participation in housework and childcare, with only 15% of men contributing significantly to the housework and 30% to the childcare.

Survey research on conjugal roles

Larger-scale research using survey methods provides more reliable data on the **division of labour** within the home. The British Social Attitudes Survey has collected data over a number of years and found some shift away from traditional roles in the 1980s and early 1990s. However, in more recent years there has been little change. In 1994 women always or usually did the laundry in 81% of households; by 2006 this had fallen just 4% to 77%.

% saying task 'usually or always' done by women	1994	2002	2006
Laundry	81	81	77
Shopping for groceries	42	46	42

Essential notes

Ann Oakley was a pioneering feminist sociologist who was the first to study housework systematically. She clearly showed the limitations of the work of Young and Willmott, who could be accused of putting forward **malestream** (mainstream, **patriarchal**) views. This research is dated now but more recent research provides some evidence that inequalities still exist.

Examiners' notes

Examiners will always be impressed with methodological evaluations of research. When using this or other survey research it is worthwhile mentioning that the reliability of the research is always questionable. For example, it has been demonstrated that men and women often given different answers when asked about who does household tasks, so it is difficult to know how reliable any set of figures is.

Table 12
Gender and domestic tasks –
1994–2006 in Britain

Childcare

Mary Boulton (1983) argues that who does which task does not adequately represent the burden of responsibility within households. She argues that even when men help more with childcare it is still mothers who take the main responsibility for their children and who have to prioritize their children above other aspects of their lives. The National Child Development Survey (1996) found it was still very unusual for fathers to take prime responsibility for childcare.

Time

Another way to study gender roles is to examine time spent on different tasks. This gives an indication as to whether men or women spend more time on paid and unpaid work.

Gershuny (1999) examined data from 1974–5 and 1997 to look at long-term trends. He found there had been a gradual shift towards men doing a higher proportion of housework, but in 1997 women continued to do more than 60% of the domestic work even when both partners were working.

The British Time Use Survey (2005) found that women spent a total of 3 hours 32 minutes per day on housework and childcare whereas men spent on average 1 hour 56 minutes on these tasks. Men did however spend more time on paid employment. Nevertheless, on average, men had one hour 32 minutes per day more leisure time than women. The difference was less great for cohabiting men and women (because men living without a partner tend to have more leisure time than women without a partner since they are less likely to be responsible for children).

Table 13 below shows average minutes per person per day spent on various activities by sex.

2005	Male	Female
Cooking, washing up	27	54
Cleaning, tidying	13	47
Washing clothes	4	18
Repairs and gardening	23	11
Caring for own children	15	32
Paid work	211	132
Watching TV & Video	170	145

Conclusion

The evidence suggests there continue to be significant differences in the conjugal roles of husband and wife although the degree of inequality may be reducing over time. Men continue to do fewer household tasks, take less responsibility for childcare and have more leisure time than women.

Table 13
Time spent on main activities with rates of participation by sex

Conjugal roles, power and emotion work

Power and decision-making

The most common way to measure **power** in households is through an examination of decision-making.

A study by Hardill et al. (1997) examined power in dual-earner households in Nottingham using interviews. Households were classified into those where the husband's career took precedence in making major decisions, those where the wife's career took precedence, and those where neither career was deemed more important than the other. In 19 households the man's career came first, in five the woman's career came first and in six neither was prioritized. Thus men continued to be dominant in the majority of households.

Power and money

Power can also be measured in terms of control over money in the household. Jan Pahl (1989) studied 102 couples with children, and classified households into four types as shown in table 14.

Pattern of management	Number of households	Type of decision-making	Degree of inequality
Husband-controlled pooling	39	Money was shared but the husband had the dominant role in choosing how it was spent	Gives men greater power
Wife-controlled pooling	27	Money was shared but the wife had the dominant role in choosing how it was spent	Gives women greater power
Husband control	22	Husband usually had the only or main wage and gave his wife housekeeping money or allowance	Usually leads to male dominance
Wife control	14	Wife had overall control of the finances, perhaps giving her husband an allowance. Most typical in low income households which relied upon benefits	Appears to give women more power but in many cases they are struggling to pay the bills on low income making financial management a burden

Table 14
Control over money in households – Jan Pahl

Pahl found that wife-controlled pooling led to the most equal relationships but this pattern is most often found in low income households. Only just over a quarter of the couples had a system that was fairly equal, suggesting men continue to be dominant.

Research by Laurie and Gershuny (2000) using data from the British Household Panel Survey (1991 and 1995) showed movement away from the housekeeping allowance system which tends to make males dominant. Over the period the proportion saying that male and female partners had an equal say rose from 65% to 70%. Equality was more likely where women had high earnings, but overall men still have more economic power.

Conjugal roles and emotion work

Jean Duncombe and Dennis Marsden (1995) believe that any measurement of inequality within households must take account of **emotion work**. Emotion work involves thinking about the happiness and emotional well-being of others and acting in ways which will be of emotional benefit to others. It might include:

- complimenting other people
- smoothing over arguments
- buying presents and cards for birthdays
- planning activities that others will enjoy
- smiling at a baby.

Duncombe and Marsden believe that women perform a **triple shift**, not only doing most of the housework and childcare, and doing their fair share of paid work, but also doing the vast majority of the emotion work. Their study involving interviews with 40 couples found that many women were dissatisfied with their partner's emotional input. Many believed that their emotion work helped to keep the family together.

Lesbian households

Gillian Dunne (1999) studied roles within lesbian households in many of which there was a dependent child. Unlike heterosexual households, responsibility for childcare was fairly equally shared rather than being largely the responsibility of one partner. Household tasks were also fairly equally shared in more than 80% of the cases studied.

Dunne concludes that masculine and feminine roles in society tend to lead to hierarchical relationships and male dominance. Without these **gender roles** greater equality is much easier to achieve.

Conjugal roles: conclusion

Most of the evidence suggests that women are still far from achieving equality within marriage in Britain today.

- They still do the majority of the housework.
- They still take the main responsibility for childcare.
- They still have less time for leisure than their male partners.

However, there is some evidence of change over time, and in terms of the total amount of hours per day spent on work of one kind or another differences between males and females are no longer that great.

Examiners' notes

This is a large-scale study so the data is quite reliable. It hints at the variety of relationships within households so remember to point out that there are a wide range of different arrangements affected by factors such as class and how much paid work each partner does.

Essential notes

This study and the concepts of the triple shift and emotion work have been widely quoted and it is important to learn them for the exam. The concept of emotion work adds an extra dimension to our understanding of family life although some people may feel that it is stretching the definition of work.

Domestic violence and abuse

Types and definition

The main types of violence and abuse in families are:

- Violence and abuse perpetrated by one adult partner against another (usually called **domestic violence**).
- Violence and abuse perpetrated by adults against children (child abuse).

The Home Office (2000) defines domestic violence as 'any violence between current or former partners in an intimate relationship wherever and whenever it occurs. The violence may include physical, sexual, emotional, or financial abuse'.

This broad definition is generally given for **domestic abuse**. A narrower definition of domestic violence includes physical and sexual violence but not emotional or financial abuse.

The extent of domestic violence and abuse

The British Crime Survey produces figures on domestic violence and other forms of abuse. The 2009–10 survey found in the previous 12 months in England and Wales:

- four women in every thousand were a victim of domestic violence
- two men in every thousand were a victim of domestic violence.

Fig 10 shows that domestic violence rose considerably between 1981 and 1996, although it has gradually declined since then.

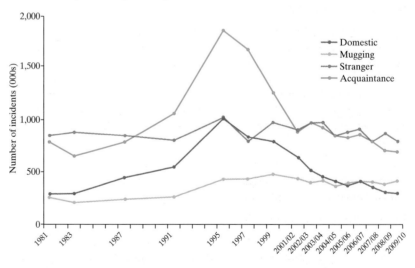

Fig 10
Domestic violence compared with other crime trends in England and Wales, 1981–2010

This survey also found that 7% of women aged 16 to 59 were victims of domestic abuse (physical, emotional, psychological or financial abuse) in the previous year compared with 4% of men.

Research by Nazroo (1999) suggests that domestic violence perpetrated by men against women tends to be more serious than that perpetrated by women on men, and women are likely to be much more fearful of the violence than men are.

The British Crime Survey is based on a large sample of over 40,000 so it is quite reliable, but it only covers England and Wales and people aged 16 or over so the scope of the statistics is somewhat limited. The validity of the data may be open to question since it can be a matter of interpretation whether abuse has taken place.

Explanations of domestic violence and abuse
Feminism

Radical feminists, such as Erin Pizzey (1974), see domestic violence as resulting from **patriarchy**. In a male-dominated or patriarchal society, men use violence or the threat of violence in order to control women. Pizzey also argues that domestic violence is widely tolerated and often not seen as a serious crime. Patriarchal values lead to female partners being seen as essentially the property of their male partners, and therefore using violence to control them is seen as partially acceptable.

Fiona Brookman (2008) believes that the nature of **masculinity** is partly to blame. In our culture masculinity values control over others, so men can resort to violence if they feel they are losing control over their female partner. Her research was based on in-depth interviewing with violent men.

A problem with this approach is that it does not explain the existence of domestic violence perpetrated by women against men. Social attitudes may also have changed since Pizzey was writing, with domestic violence now seen as less socially acceptable by the public, and more likely to result in prosecution by the police.

Dysfunctional families

Some conservative commentators associated with the views of the **New Right** believe that domestic violence takes place in **dysfunctional families**, that is, families which do not function well. Their view is that violence results from the instability of families caused by factors such as increasing **cohabitation** and **divorce**, and the decline in moral standards in some families, particularly those from lower social classes. This view suggests that feminists exaggerate male violence and underestimate female violence.

This approach is criticized by feminists who believe that male violence against women is both much more serious and much more common than female violence against men.

Emotional intensity and family life

Anthony Giddens (2006) argues that it is the nature of family life that makes domestic violence quite common. Family life is characterized by 'emotional intensity and personal intimacy', meaning that it is normally charged with strong emotions, often 'mixing love and hate'. In these circumstances, even minor arguments can escalate into acts of violence. The increasing isolation of the **nuclear family** from **extended kinship networks** may be increasing this intensity.

A problem with this approach is that it does not explain why violence is common in some families but not others.

Essential notes

It is useful to comment that these figures may underestimate the true extent of domestic violence and abuse, since many victims may be unwilling to admit that it has taken place.

Examiners' notes

It is useful to comment here that **liberal feminists** recognize that there may have been some improvements in the treatment of victims of domestic abuse and violence. Referring to different feminist perspectives can help to get you in the top mark band.

Examiners' notes

To critique this view you can suggest that there is little evidence to support it and it may be based largely on the political views of the writers.

Examiners' notes

You can gain extra credit by making reference to specific research on changes in extended family networks, either to support or criticize this view (see pp 16–17).

The social construction of childhood

The dominant framework

Michael Wyness (2006) says that commonsense thinking sees childhood as 'a natural and inevitable phase of life that we all go through'. It is seen as a biological state due to the physical and mental immaturity of children. Therefore, childhood should be the same across different cultures and over time.

Prout and James (1997) see this view as the **dominant framework**.

Child	Adult
Nature	Culture
Simple	Complex
Amoral	Moral
Asocial	Social
Person-in-waiting	Personhood
Becoming	Being

Table 15
The dominant framework

The key features of this framework for Wyness are:

1. Childhood and adulthood are seen as opposites, and childhood is seen as lacking the key attributes of being a person which are attained in adulthood.
2. Children are not seen in their own rights but in terms of what they will become later, that is, they are seen as future adults.
3. Children are regarded as at the earliest or most primitive stage of individuality.

Prout sees this view of children as the product of **modernity**. In modernity adults are associated with **rationality** and children are associated with a lack of rationality.

The dominant framework is backed up by developmentalism in which childhood is seen as a series of stages through which children develop as they get closer to adulthood.

Childhood as a social construction

Many sociologists challenge the dominant framework by claiming that childhood is a **social construction**. From this viewpoint it is not a natural, biological stage in development but a social role which is learnt through **socialization** and which varies from society to society and over time. For example:

- In some societies children do a considerable amount of paid work.
- Amnesty International (2007) estimates there are 300,000 child soldiers in the world.
- Pilcher (1995) identifies wide cultural variations in the role of children. Samoan children are expected to take part in physical and dangerous work, and in Tikopia in the Pacific children are not expected to obey adults.

Essential notes

Useful links can be made here with the theories of modernity and changes in relationship put forward by Beck and Giddens (see p 21).

Essential notes

The idea of a social construction is a crucial one and may need defining in the exam. When sociologists say something is a social construction they mean that it is shaped by a society's culture even when people might believe that it is natural and is not influenced by social factors.

Key study
Philippe Ariès – centuries of childhood

Ariès (1973) pioneered the idea of childhood as a social construction. According to his research, in mediaeval times (roughly the 12th to 16th centuries) modern conceptions of childhood did not exist. For example:

- **Chronological age** (the number of years since you were born) was not considered significant.
- Children often died before reaching adulthood and so were regarded as being less important than they are today.
- Parents kept the mourning for children who died to a minimum.
- Children were expected to work as soon as they were physically capable of doing so.
- Both adults and children spent time on play and often played the same games.
- There were few specialist clothes for children so they dressed like little adults.
- Children were not regarded as being especially innocent, nor protected from exposure to sexuality.

Examiners' notes

This is the most important study that needs to be quoted if you are asked questions about the nature of childhood or changes in childhood over long periods of time. Some sociologists don't agree with Ariès about the exact reasons for changes in childhood or the timing of the changes (see the evaluation below) but it's widely accepted that his general view is broadly correct.

Evaluation

Ariès has been criticized for claiming that there was no concept of childhood in mediaeval times; others believe the conception of childhood was simply different. He has also been criticized for basing his research on a small sample of untypical French aristocratic families.

The emergence of childhood

Ariès believes that towards the end of the mediaeval period **modern** conceptions of childhood began to appear as church leaders began to see children as 'fragile creatures who needed to be safeguarded and reformed'. The introduction of schools, in which separate age groups were taught and children were segregated from the adult world, helped introduce the idea of childhood as a distinct phase of life in which children had to be kept innocent and protected from the adult world.

Compared with mediaeval times, society became more **child-centred** with the well-being and development of children seen as very important. In the 20th century, sciences such as psychology, psychoanalysis and paediatrics were developed, and these created specialists who emphasized the needs of children.

Examiners' notes

The idea of child-centredness is an important one for questions about changing roles within the family because it implies changes in the roles of parents and children.

As modern attitudes to childhood developed, children were:
- treated differently according to their chronological age
- seen as important and in need of protection
- strongly mourned if they died
- not required to work
- given specialist games and toys which adults did not take part in
- given distinctive clothes
- seen as asexual and kept away from exposure to sexuality.

Changing childhood

Edward Shorter – childhood and the modern family

Edward Shorter (1976) uses a wider range of evidence than Ariès, and from a greater variety of countries, to describe and explain the development of childhood.

Shorter links the development of childhood to motherhood. According to his research, in the 17th and early 18th centuries mothers showed little interest in bonding with their children and could handle children quite roughly. Children were usually left to cry rather than picked up and comforted.

Attitudes started changing in the 18th century because:

1. The idea of romantic love began to develop and children were seen as the products of a special relationship.
2. Philosophers such as Jean Jacques Rousseau popularized the idea that children were born good and could become reasoning adults if successfully **socialized**.
3. New ideas began to circulate on the best ways to raise children.

By the 20th century, being a 'good' mother was considered very important and the harshness of early centuries was replaced with a desire to nurture children. Mothers developed a sacrificial role in which their children's lives were more important than their own.

Evaluation

Shorter assumes that changing ideas were largely responsible for changes in childhood. However some sociologists believe that other factors were more important.

Other explanations of the development of childhood

- Neil Postman (1982) sees the explanation for changes in childhood as lying in technological change. The printing press developed in the late 15th century and as a result learning to read became increasingly important in society. Learning to read was a gradual process and required extended schooling of children. This led to the separation of adults and children and the idea that children had to pass through age-related stages as they progressed towards adulthood.
- Other sociologists believe that Postman attaches too much importance to a single cause of the changes. Jane Pilcher (1995) also sees employment legislation as important. In the 19th century, Factory Acts banned children from an increasing number of workplaces, and this laid the foundation for the separation of adults and children in schools. Pilcher believes that the development of childhood varied for different groups, such as different social classes and boys and girls, but eventually the modern idea of childhood developed for all children.

Examiners' notes

You can use Shorter to contrast with Ariès (see p 53) in answering questions on the social construction of childhood or changes in childhood. Shorter provides a more developed explanation than Ariès and uses a greater variety of evidence, but Shorter himself has been criticized (see below)

Examiners' notes

Evaluation of these theories is really important to get into the higher mark bands on essay questions. Contrasting the competing viewpoints is an effective way to evaluate.

Childhood and modernity

Christopher Jenks (2005) believes that the development of modern childhood involves a shift from the **Dionysian image of the child** to the **Apollonian image**.

- The Dionysian image assumes that children naturally pursue their own pleasure, which can lead to their acting in evil ways. They therefore require close control and strict moral guidance to grow up to be moral adults. From this viewpoint there was little sentimentality about children so that having young children working in mines and factories and as chimney sweeps was quite acceptable.
- The Apollonian image developed from the middle of the 18th century, based on the ideas of Rousseau. It believed that children are born good but this good side must be coaxed out of them sympathetically. This thinking resulted in the idea of child-centred education and the banning of paid work for young children. Harsh physical punishment was replaced by monitoring and careful control of where children were allowed to go and what they were allowed to do. For example, much of children's time was spent in school behind school desks.

Childhood and postmodernity

Jenks believes that **postmodern** childhood has developed. In postmodern societies identities have been destabilized so that people no longer have a secure, grounded sense of who they are. Class solidarity has broken down and family life is insecure with frequent **divorce**. In these circumstances children have become the final source of **primary relationships** – the most fulfilling and unconditional relationships. Wives and husbands and partners have become disposable, but children are not and the parent–child bond is therefore the most important in society. This intensifies the sense that children need to be protected, and helps to explain the growing anxiety about child abuse. Children become subject to increased surveillance because parents are more fearful for their children and determined to protect them.

Evaluation

Jenks has been criticized for ignoring evidence that mothers place increasing emphasis on careers rather than children, but research by Gatrell (2005) found than many parents do see relationships with children as more important than their relationship with their partner.

Examiners' notes

These concepts might seem rather obscure and remote from social life, but they do underpin attitudes to children and you can certainly get credit for using concepts such as these.

Essential notes

Jenks' views are very similar to those of Anthony Giddens (see p 21) and it is worth mentioning this. Both Jenks and Giddens offer rather generalized views without much research to back them up. Both of them neglect the variations in relationships within families, for example between different ethnic groups.

Essential notes

Postman's ideas have some similarity with the views of the **New Right** that traditional family life is under threat because morality has been undermined in a more liberal society. You could critique Postman by arguing that he exaggerates the degree to which children were sheltered from adult life and sexuality in previous eras and that he provides little evidence to support the view that they were sheltered in this way.

Contemporary perspectives on childhood

Neil Postman: the disappearance of childhood

Postman (1994) claims that the distinction between childhood and adulthood has been eroded in recent years so that childhood no longer exists as a distinct stage in the **life course**.

He explains the disappearance in the following ways:

1. The growth of the mass media has exposed children to the adult world. It is easy for them to access images of sex and they can view suffering and death on television news programmes. More recently, the internet provides children with access to images and information from which they were previously sheltered.
2. The difference between adulthood and childhood is increasingly blurred. Examples of this include:
- children dressing in more adult and sometimes more sexualized ways
- adults trying to dress and act in more youthful ways
- the lack of a clear-cut transition to adulthood as adolescence is extended and young people often delay getting a job, setting up their own home, getting married and having children.

Children as consumers

Another way in which the distinctiveness of childhood may be disappearing is in the increasing participation of children in consumption. Research by Evans and Chandler (2006) found there was strong peer pressure amongst children to persuade their parents to buy them the latest designer goods. Marketing and adverts are often aimed at children and encourage participation in consumer society.

Jenks – the continuing distinctiveness of childhood

Jenks (2005) accepts that there is increasing confusion over the nature of childhood but he does not believe that it is disappearing as a distinct stage in the life course. He does, though, agree that there has been increased concern about the loss of innocence amongst children since the 1993 murder of the toddler James Bulger by two older children in Liverpool.

Nevertheless, Jenks points out that children continue to be highly regulated and restricted by laws which control behaviour in public spaces, the consumption of alcohol and cigarettes, education, sexuality, political rights and so on. Table 16 below shows the ages at which various activities are legal in the UK.

Essential notes

The Bulger case produced particular anxiety because it involved extreme violence by children against children. However, you should remember that it was only one case and violence such as this is very rare, so it probably says more about increasing levels of anxiety in society than the actual changing behaviour of the vast majority of children.

Table 16
Legal ages in the UK

At any age you can:	At 5 you can:	At 10 you are:	At 12 you can:	At 13 you can:
Agree to or refuse medical treatment. Open a bank account. Ask to see school records. Have confidential contraceptive treatment.	See a U or PG film by yourself.	Legally responsible for any crimes.	Buy a pet. See a 12-rated film by yourself.	Work part time.

At 14 you can:	At 16 you can:	At 17 you can:	At 18 you can:	At 21 you can:
Go into a pub alone for soft drinks with the landlord's consent. Work in a market.	Have a beer with a meal in a restaurant. Buy lottery tickets. Marry or join the armed forces with parental agreement. Leave school. Have sex. Buy cigarettes. Ride a moped up to 50 cc.	Give blood. Drive a motorcycle, car or van. Apply for a helicopter pilot's licence.	Buy alcohol. Serve on a jury. Leave home, join the armed forces or marry without parental permission. Buy fireworks. Place bets. Own land. Drive smaller lorries. Vote.	Become a local councillor or MP. Drive larger lorries.

Theoretical approaches to childhood: the conventional approach

The conventional theoretical approach to children and childhood reflects the views of **functionalists** and the New Right. This sees children as a vulnerable group in need of protection from exposure to adult life. It views children as growing up too quickly and therefore being likely to engage in inappropriate behaviour.

An example of this approach is provided by Melanie Phillips (1997), a right-wing commentator who believes that parenting culture in Britain is failing children. She claims that:

1. Liberal ideas of parenting have given children too many rights and powers and have prevented parents from disciplining their children (e.g. through smacking) to ensure that they show respect for parents and others in authority.
2. **Peer groups** and the mass media have come to have more influence on children than parents and teachers, leading to children losing their innocence and becoming sexualized at a younger age (e.g. the increase in pregnancies under 16).

Berry Mayall – the new sociology of children

Berry Mayall (2004) has a very different view to Phillips, arguing that most ideas on childhood and children are **adultist** – they see children from an adult point of view and are biased in favour of adults at the expense of children. According to Mayall this ignores the rights of children and underestimates the ability of children to think and act for themselves.

Now that women have achieved greater rights, children are the final group who are denied rights to make their own decisions. Children have no right to shape their own schooling and have little influence on policies which affect them. This exposes children to danger, for example making it easy for adults to abuse them.

By giving children more of a voice in policies which affect them they will be better served by social policies and less vulnerable to abuse.

Essential notes

As noted earlier, these sort of New Right views tie in with some of Postman's ideas.

Examiners' notes

Mayall is useful for adding a critical view which can be contrasted with all the other approaches to childhood and children. You could even suggest that her pioneering perspective will gain increasing acceptance in sociology, rather like the way in which feminism has gained acceptance for female viewpoints. Therefore, try to use this material in answering questions about the changing roles of children.

Demography and the birth rate

Demography

The study of demography examines factors affecting the total size of the population in a country. Total population size is shaped by the following factors:

1. The **birth rate** – the number of live births per thousand of the population per year.
2. The **fertility rate** – the number of live births per thousand women aged 15 to 44 per year.
3. The **death rate** – the number of deaths per thousand of the population per year.
4. **Migration** – the number of people entering a country (immigration) and the number of people leaving the country (emigration). **Net migration** refers to the difference between the numbers entering and leaving the country.

The population of the UK

In 1801 the UK had a population of 10.5 million. By 1901 it had risen to 37 million, by 1971 to just under 56 million, and it is estimated to reach over 62 million in 2011.

Fig 11 shows the total number of births and deaths in the UK since 1901. There have been fewer deaths than births in the UK in every year since 1901, with the exception of 1976. This has meant that the population has risen largely as a result of natural increase for most of the 20th century, although migration has also played a part (see pp 64–65). Natural increase occurs when the number of births exceeds the number of deaths. In the 1950s, for example, natural change accounted for 98% of population growth; however, between 2001 and 2004 net migration explained approximately two-thirds of the increasing UK population.

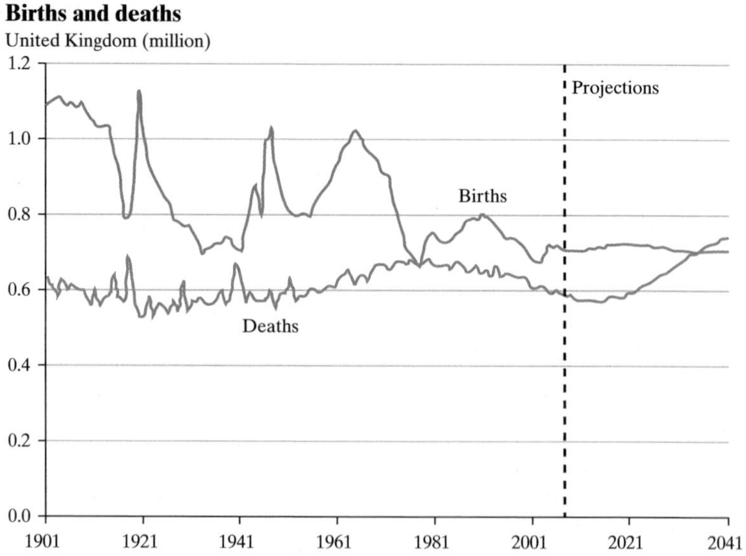

Births and deaths
United Kingdom (million)

Fig 11
UK births and deaths from 1901

The birth rate

There has been a long-term decline in the number of births in the UK and also in the birth rate.

In 2008 there were 790 000 live births in the UK compared with 1 093 000 in 1901 when the population was significantly lower. Although there have been fluctuations in the birth rate, which increased with a 'baby boom' after both the First and Second World Wars (partly because some people had delayed starting families until after the ending of the wars), over the long term the birth rate has been declining.

The fertility rate

Much of the decline in the birth rate has been the result of a declining fertility rate – women are choosing to have fewer children. The total fertility rate (the number of children each woman has) has declined from 3.5 in 1900 to 1.7 in 1997. It rose slightly to 1.94 in 2009.

This recent rise in fertility is partly due to patterns of migration with immigrants to the UK tending to have slightly larger families than non-immigrants. The recent rise has also been explained in terms of rising fertility rates in older women, some of which may be due to improvements in fertility treatments such as IVF.

Examiners' notes

If you are asked for a long answer about reasons for changes in population size, you will need to discuss births, deaths and migration to give an overall picture.

Reasons for the long-term decline in birth and fertility rates

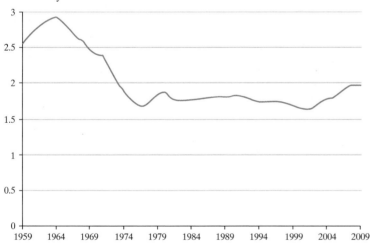

Total Fertility Rate

Fig 12
Falling fertility rates from 1959 to 2009 in the UK

Changes in gender roles

A major part of the decline can be explained in terms of women choosing to have fewer children. As their role in society has changed, many women are choosing to delay childbearing and to limit the number of children they have. Factors include:

- Improved contraception from the 1960s, which gave women more control over their own fertility.
- Easier access to abortion.

- Women are less likely to get married than in the past and cohabiting women are less likely to have children than married women.
- An increase in the number of women in paid employment, particularly after marriage, so that more women delay or limit childbearing to fit in with careers.
- In **dual-earner families** it is more difficult to combine work with care of a large number of children.
- More opportunities for women in employment because of the growth of the service sector.
- Greater legal equality for women, such as the Equal Pay Act (1970) which has made working more worthwhile.
- Improved female performance in education and increasing educational opportunities.

Examiners' notes

Questions on the birth or fertility rate are quite straightforward, but including this type of theory can help get you into the top mark band.

Examiners' notes

You can answer questions on reasons for changes in the birth rate and in the fertility rate using essentially the same material.

A decline in the birth and fertility rates may be largely a matter of choice, particularly the choice of women. Also, women who delay the birth of their first child until they are relatively old may not remain fertile long enough to have large numbers of children. However, fertility rates amongst older age groups have been rising.

Falling infant mortality

The **infant mortality rate** (the number of children dying before their first birthday per thousand live births) has fallen dramatically as a result of factors such as rising living standards, improved hygiene and sanitation, improvements in healthcare, and improved monitoring of child welfare as a result of the development of the welfare state.

Geographers explain that these circumstances lead to a **demographic revolution** in which birth and fertility rates fall because women no longer feel they need to have a large number of children to protect against the risk of infant mortality.

Children as an economic burden

In the early 19th century children were often seen as an economic asset because it was possible to send them out to work to contribute to the family income at a relatively early age. However, legislation has gradually banned or restricted the opportunities for children to work, and the length of time children spend in schooling has gradually increased. This has made children economically dependent upon their parents for longer and means they represent an economic cost rather than an economic asset. In addition, the development of welfare provision for the elderly has made parents less dependent upon children for care and support in old age. As people expect and desire rising living standards, then there is a greater disincentive to have large numbers of children.

Changing attitudes

As pp 52–67 show, attitudes towards children and childhood have changed. Families and society in general have become more **child-centred**, more concerned with the well-being of children, than they were in the past. As social norms about what constitutes adequate childcare have changed, the time and costs involved in raising children have increased. This has further reduced the economic attractiveness of having large numbers of children. Instead, parents are more likely to concentrate their efforts on raising a small number of children as well as they can.

Beck and Beck-Gernsheim (1995) believe that these changes are linked to a process of **individualization**. People no longer have to follow traditional norms and values and instead make their own decisions. These decisions include: whether or not to get married, whether to stay married and whether to have children. Uncertainty and the risk of relationship breakdown make people wary of having too many children. Ironically, however, the children that people do have become increasingly important to them since parent–child relationships are permanent while marriages may be temporary.

The effects of changes in fertility

Changes in fertility can have a number of consequences for society. These include.

- Changes in the **dependency ratio**. The dependency ratio is the ratio between the economically productive part of the population and non-workers, or dependents, such as children and the elderly. Falling fertility rates reduce the number of dependent children in the short term but in the long term lead to fewer adults of working age, which can increase the proportion of the population who are dependent.
- Effects on public services such as education. Falling numbers of births can lead to the closure of maternity units and schools, which can create problems if the birth rate increases later.
- Falling fertility can contribute further to changes in **gender roles**, giving women more time to devote to their careers and therefore contributing to greater equality in conjugal relationships.

The death rate

Changes in the death rate

- Since 1901 the total number of deaths in the UK has remained relatively stable at around the 600 000 mark. In 1901 there were 632 000 deaths and 574 700 in 2007. The peak year for deaths since 1901 was in 1918 when approximately 690 000 people died, with an influenza outbreak and the First World War claiming many of those lives.
- Since 1901, however, the UK population has increased, therefore the death rate has fallen.
- In 1900–02 **death rates** stood at 18.4 per thousand per year, by 1976 this was 12.1. Between 1976 and 2007 death rates fell by more than 22% to 9.4 per thousand per year.
- **Infant mortality rates** (number of babies dying before the age of one per thousand babies born alive per year) have declined even quicker than overall death rates, falling by two thirds from 14.5 in 1976 to 4.8 in 2007.
- Falling death rates are reflected in rising **life expectancy**. In 1901 life expectancy at birth was 45 for boys and 49 for girls; by 2009 this had reached 77.7 years for boys and 81.9 for girls.
- Death rates and life expectancy vary between social groups and places. For example, government statistics showed that in 2007 infant mortality was more than twice as high in children of married couples from the lowest class (routine occupations), at 6.3%, than it was for children from the highest class (higher managerial and large employers), at 2.7%

Reasons for the declining death rate
Developments in medicine

A variety of researchers have found that well over half of the decline in the death rate since the 19th century has been due to a decrease in infectious diseases such as tuberculosis, measles, whooping cough and diphtheria. The most obvious reason for this decline is medical advances. From the 1920s vaccines were introduced to combat many of these diseases, and antibiotics were introduced from the 1930s. However, Thomas McKeown (1979) argues that most of the fall in deaths from infectious diseases took place before the discovery of vaccinations and antibiotics. He believes that improved nutrition was the most important factor in reducing death rates from such diseases, with improvements in hygiene accounting for about 20% of the decline.

More recently, death rates from the so-called 'diseases of affluence' such as cancer and heart disease have increased. For these diseases medical knowledge and improved medical services have made a difference. For example, deaths from heart disease have decreased partly as a result of the availability of better drugs and operations such as heart bypass.

Improvements in maternity care since the establishment of the NHS in 1949 have probably made a significant difference to infant mortality rates.

Nutrition and living standards

Studies by Rowntree and others (1899, 1950) demonstrated a rapid decline in **absolute poverty** (absolute poverty involves a lack of the basic necessities of life such as food and shelter). Increases in living standards have allowed significant improvements in diet throughout the population. Better nutrition helps to increase resistance to infectious diseases.

Welfare, health and environment

At the same time as individual living standards have risen, government provision of welfare and health has improved.

- In the late 19th and early 20th centuries significant improvements were made in the water supply and sewage disposal.
- In 1914 free school meals were introduced for those who could not afford them.
- Sickness benefit was introduced in 1911.
- After the Bcveridge Report of 1944, the range of welfare provision expanded and became more universally available. It provided protection against risk factors such as old age through pensions, and low income through housing benefits, unemployment benefit and the benefit now called Income Support.

The table below shows the infant mortality rate in England and Wales for 2007.

Infant mortality: by socio-economic classification 2007		
England & Wales	**Rates per 1,000 live births**	
	Inside marriage	**Outside marriage**
Large employers and higher managerial	2.7	3.3
Higher professional	3.1	3.9
Lower managerial and professional	3.3	3.5
Intermediate occupations	4.5	3.9
Small employers and own account workers	3.9	4.0
Lower supervisory and technical	3.8	4.1
Semi-routine occupations	6.0	6.0
Routine occupations	6.3	5.5
All	4.2	5.0

Table 17
Infant mortality rate in England and Wales, 2007

Conclusion

Most of the reduction in the death rate is due to improvements in living standards and the expansion of welfare although medical advances have come to play a greater role in recent years as the significance of infectious diseases has declined. The continued inequalities in death rates between social classes show that economic and social factors continue to be important.

Essential notes

This doesn't mean that there is no longer any poverty. **Relative poverty** (that is, being poor relative to other people in a society) remains a major problem and research shows that it lowers life expectancy. Absolute poverty lowers it even more, and is still experienced by a few: for example, some of the homeless.

Examiners' notes

Don't forget to learn some of these details, but be careful not to use older examples if the question specifies a shorter timeframe (for example, the last thirty years).

Migration
Patterns of migration

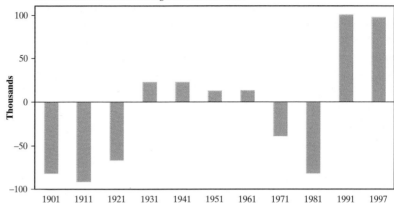

UK annual net international migrations 1901 to 1997.

Essential notes

It is important to emphasize that there have been long periods when there were more emigrants from Britain than immigrants to Britain, but recently the reverse has been true.

Fig 13 shows that:

- In the early decades of the 20th century the UK was a net exporter of people. The majority of those leaving went to the USA, Australia, New Zealand and other colonies. Most immigrants were from Ireland. After the end of the First World War the trend reversed with many migrants returning to Britain and the immigration of eastern European Jews fleeing persecution.
- From the late 1950s immigration from the Caribbean and the Asian subcontinent increased, although in the 1970s and 1980s Britain was a net exporter of people as UK citizens left to start new lives in Australia, New Zealand and South Africa.
- In recent decades immigration has exceeded emigration despite a variety of Acts restricting the rights of Commonwealth citizens to settle in Britain. Some immigrants are asylum seekers fleeing persecution, and most recently many are from European Union countries, particularly in Eastern Europe. Some British people have emigrated to live in other European countries, often for retirement purposes. The European Union allows free movement of people within its boundaries. In 2004, the European Union was expanded to include 10 new member states including Poland. There have also been some illegal immigrants.

However, the situation is always changing and economic and other changes in Britain might change the trends in the future.

Usually migrants tend to be relatively young and they are more likely to be male than female. However, older people may also emigrate, for example British people seeking to retire in warmer countries such as France and Spain.

Factors affecting migration
Legislation and border control

Legal migration is affected by laws governing the right of people to move to other countries, while illegal migration is affected by the attempts of states to control access to their territory. For example, the UK has limited immigration from the Caribbean and Asian subcontinent due to Acts such as the 1962 and 1968 Commonwealth Immigration Acts. The 1999 Immigration and Asylum Act tightened up regulations allowing asylum seekers to settle in Britain. However, the expansion of the European Union has given more people the right to come to Britain.

Globalization

Globalization involves a process in which national boundaries become less important and interconnections between different parts of the globe become more important. With the development of mass communications, awareness and understanding of other countries and cultures has increased. With rapid, cheap and safe transport systems such as jet air travel, movement around the globe has become more affordable and easier. These factors have increased the total amount of migration in the world.

'Push' and 'pull' factors

Other factors which affect migration can be seen as 'push' and 'pull' factors.

- **'Push' factors** give people a reason to emigrate. For example, they may be fleeing war persecution, poverty or unemployment.
- **'Pull' factors** attract people to move to a particular country, for example political stability and respect for human rights, and opportunities for education, training or employment.
- A high proportion of migrants state that they move either to a particular job or to look for work.
- In 2007, more than a quarter of immigrants came to Britain in order to study. Many would later leave.
- The next most important reason is to accompany or join partners, family members or friends.
- With the importance of economic factors, the state of the economy in comparison to other economies can affect migration. For example, after 2004 there was a high rate of economic migration to the UK (which had a booming economy) from Eastern Europe (where the economies were less strong). Since the 2008/9 credit crunch and subsequent recession, many of these migrants have left Britain.

Conclusion

Given the variety of factors which can shape migration there is no guarantee that the UK will continue to be a net importer of people. However, current projections suggest that net immigration will continue to increase for a number of years to come.

Examiners' notes

Migration is a controversial and emotive issue but this shouldn't be your approach in the exam. Stick to the evidence without passing any judgement on whether migration is beneficial or not.

Examiners' notes

You must discuss both these types of factor in longer answers but it isn't really possible to say which is more important because this varies with individual circumstances.

Essential notes

Economic factors can act as both a push and a pull for migrants; for example, if there are few jobs in their country of origin but more jobs available in the country they are emigrating to.

The ageing population

Changes in the age structure

The age structure refers to the proportion of people in different age groups in a particular population. This can be represented in population pyramids (such as fig 14) which divide different segments of the population into age groups and by doing so illustrate the relative proportions of different age groups for these segments.

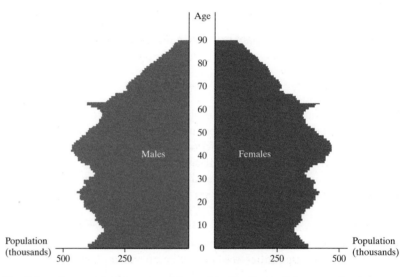

Fig 14
Population estimates UK – 2009

Traditionally, population pyramids tend to be triangular, narrowing in older age groups, but recent trends in the UK have produced an **ageing population** with a rising proportion of elderly and middle aged people and a falling proportion of children and younger adults. For example, between 1984 and 2009:

- The percentage of the population over 65 increased from 15 to 16%.
- The percentage of the population under 16 decreased from 21 to 19%.

On projected trends, by 2034, 23% of the population will be over 65, while just 18% will be under 16.

The **median** age (the age of the person in the middle of the age distribution) increased from 35 years in 1984 to 39 in 2009 and is projected to rise to 42 by 2034.

Reasons for the ageing population

The main reasons for an ageing population are:

- The falling **death rate** – people tend to survive more years after reaching adulthood, leading to a growing number of elderly in the population.
- The falling **birth rate** and **fertility rate** – children constitute a proportion of the population.

The effects of an ageing population

An ageing population can have a number of effects.

The dependency ratio

The rising proportion of the population beyond retirement age increases the economic burden on those of working age who need to pay taxes to cover the costs associated with the retired population, such as pensions and healthcare.

Effects on families

An ageing population can place extra economic, emotional and practical burdens on adults of working age who may need to care for elderly parents as well as raising children. This burden tends to fall particularly heavily on women, who usually end up being the main carers.

Government spending

Provision for the welfare of the elderly and those over pension age imposes a large burden upon the government. Relatively little in taxes is received from people who are retired but their demands on healthcare are likely to be greater than younger members of the population. In response to this problem the government in the UK has restricted the amount of support provided for care of the elderly and has started to raise retirement ages. Under the current plans, the state pension age will rise from 60 to 66 for women and from 65 to 66 for men by 2020. Between 2024 and 2046 the state pension will rise further to 68 for both men and women.

Social problems for older people

An ageing population will result in increasing numbers of households consisting of single pensioners (most often women) living alone. As pension provision is reduced and people live longer the number of retired people living in **poverty** is likely to increase.

However, these problems should not be exaggerated since the health of older groups in the population has been improving, making it possible for more people to remain economically active longer and placing less burden on health and social services.

Perspectives on old age

The functionalists Elena Cumming and William Henry (1961) see the **disengagement** of older people from society as beneficial. (Disengagement involves gradual withrawal from social roles.) If older people continue working, for example, they will block opportunities for younger people and they may become less competent in performing their roles in society.

Hockey and James (1993) argue that old age is a **social construction** and that many people above retirement age are capable of carrying out a wide range of social roles if society did not expect, and sometimes require, them to withdraw from those roles, for example to retire from work.

Examiners' notes

It is important to emphasize in answers that an ageing population can be the result of low birth and fertility rates just as much as it can be a result of increasing life expectancy.

Essential notes

See pp 58–61 and 62–63 for information covering the reasons for the falling birth rate and the falling death rate.

Essential notes

It is useful to make a link to feminism here: a number of feminists have studied the ways in which the care of elderly parents restricts the life chances of women.

Examiners' notes

The examiner will be impressed if you get some balance into your answer by showing that there are some positive aspects to the ageing population such as improvement in health.

General tips for the Families and Households exam

The Families and Households examination paper consists of five compulsory questions to be completed in one hour. The maximum mark for this paper is 60, so this is just less than one mark per minute, once you have taken off time for reading. You should not spend too long on the short questions, as the two essays are worth 24 marks each. There are a total of 12 marks for the three short questions – either 2:4:6 or 4:4:4 marks. Answers to these questions should be clear and concise.

You will be given two Items to read, to help you with some of the questions. Once you know what the questions are about, you should read the Items carefully to identify points or issues that you can use. Remember the Items are there only to provide you with a starting point; this is NOT a comprehension.

- **Question 01** is usually worth 2 marks and will ask you to explain a concept (or, sometimes, to compare two concepts for 4 marks). Give a clear explanation, not an example, and avoid using the term you are being asked about in your explanation. If there are inverted commas around the term to be explained, you should explain *all* the words *within* them.
- **Questions 02** and **03** will ask you to identify, suggest or explain two or three things. Examples could be two or three ways, reasons, problems, criticisms, factors, effects, causes etc. 'Identify' means that you need to state from your knowledge answers that are already established in sociology. 'Suggest' means that you can include any answer that you think might be appropriate or plausible. It's always a good idea to separate the two or three points you are making – this makes your answer clearer for the examiner. Try not to choose answers that overlap. As with question 01, try to be concise. One sentence is often enough for each point.
- **Question 04** is an essay question and it is free-standing. This means that there is no reference to either of the Items – all the material for the answer has to be provided by you. The question will ask you to 'examine'. This means you must look at the different aspects of an issue closely and in detail. 14 of the marks for this essay are for AO1 skills of knowledge and understanding; 10 are for AO2 skills of interpretation, application, analysis and evaluation. So although there are plenty of marks for showing your sociological knowledge, you must also make sure you include plenty of evidence of the AO2 skills.
- **Question 05** is the second essay question, but this one is connected to at least one of the Items. It will usually ask you to use the Item and therefore you will not be able to gain top marks if you do not do so. You should try to build on the Item by developing some of the ideas put forward. However, the words, 'and elsewhere' mean that you are expected to contribute a lot of your own ideas – the Item will not provide everything you need. The question will usually ask you to 'assess'. Assessment involves evaluation and judgement, so you must therefore make sure that you are analytical and evaluative in your answer. Only 10 of the marks for this essay are for AO1 skills and 14 marks are for AO2 skills.

When writing each of the essays you should look back regularly to the question. Make sure you have obeyed all of the instructions and covered all of the issues included in the question. Some essays have two or more parts. You will not gain top marks if you do not deal with each part. It's also very important to focus on the question set. Do not be tempted to write an essay about all you know on the topic in question, or to spend time writing at a tangent to the question – try to use your material to focus on the issues.

Families and Households (sample exam paper 1)

Read Items 1A and 1B below and answer parts (01) to (05) that follow.

Item 1A

Many sociologists argue that laws and government policies have always had an effect on family life, sometimes restricting people's actions and sometimes giving the family much-needed support. Policies often reflect a particular view of how the family should be and therefore encourage certain types of family or household. For example, the New Right argue that the welfare benefits currently given to single mothers should be cut back because they encourage dependency on the state.

Item 1B

Functionalist sociologists see the family as a vital social institution. They believe it carries out a number of essential functions, both for individuals and for society as a whole. In particular, the family is viewed as the most important agent for maintaining stability, producing the next generation, and carrying out primary socialization.

However, other sociologists suggest that this functionalist view paints a picture that is too rosy. For example, Marxist and feminist sociologists argue that it ignores the more negative aspects of family life; other sociologists argue that the functionalist view does not take enough account of family variation and change.

Questions

01 Explain what is meant by 'primary socialization' (**Item 1B**, line 5). [**2 marks**]

02 Identify **two** laws or government policies that may affect roles and relationships between couples, apart from that referred to in **Item 1A.** [**4 marks**]

03 Suggest **three** reasons for changes in the position of children in the last hundred years. [**6 marks**]

04 Examine the factors that have affected the domestic division of labour and power between couples. [**24 marks**]

05 Using material from **Item 1B** and elsewhere, assess the contribution of functionalist theories to an understanding of the family. [**24 marks**]

Grade A answer

01 *Explain what is meant by 'primary socialization' (Item 1, line 5).*
[**2 marks**]

> Primary socialization is the process by which a person learns a culture, and it is taught to a child in the first few years of life. The main agent of primary socialization is the family; they teach children the basic norms of socially acceptable behaviour, crucial to a child's development and reinforced in secondary socialization.

A good answer. The candidate has explained both 'primary' and 'socialization' appropriately: the first stage, within the family, of the process of learning the culture of society.
Mark 2/2

02 *Identify two laws or government policies that may affect roles and relationships between couples, apart from that referred to in Item 1A.*
[**4 marks**]

> One government policy which may have affected roles and relationships between couples is the 2004 civil partnership law. It gave gay couples the same rights as heterosexual couples; that they could have a civil partnership and adopt children. As a result an increasing number of people are in gay relationships.
>
> Another law which may have affected roles and relationships of couples is the Equal Pay Act. This gave women the same opportunities as men in employment. This made women less dependent and changed traditional gender roles, as many women and men were equal in the world of work.

Two appropriate examples are suggested of laws that may affect couples' roles and relationships: on civil partnerships and equal pay. Possible effects on roles and relationships are suggested.

Other appropriate answers might include: divorce law, reproductive technology, child benefit.
Mark 4/4

03 *Suggest three reasons for changes in the position of children in the last hundred years.* [**6 marks**]

> The position of children in the last hundred years has improved as they were once 'seen but not heard'; however, they are now more important to the family. One reason for this could be the emergence of a child-centred society due to a higher standard of living and nutrition. This allowed child mortality rates to decline, meaning that parents had a greater expectation of their children living, meaning that they may form a better bond with them.
>
> Due to technology, parents are now able to limit the number of children they have, meaning that they can have fewer children but invest more love, socialization and protection in those children.
>
> The third reason for changes in the position of children is education. Children would have once been entered into the world of work at a very young age, and looked upon as 'young adults'.

Four appropriate answers have been suggested but only three are needed: growth of child-centredness; higher standard of living; the decline in child mortality rates; smaller families. The answers in the first paragraph could have been clearer, set out as three separate points.

The final point about compulsory schooling is not needed but would have gained only one mark, as it is only partially explained.
Mark 6/6

04 *Examine the factors that have affected the domestic division of labour and power between couples.* [**24 marks**]

The domestic division of labour is the distribution of domestic tasks, e.g. washing, ironing, childcare, between a couple. In the past these were female tasks, part of the housewife role, and functionalist sociologists saw this as the natural way things should be. However in recent years the domestic division of labour within the family seems to have become more equal, so men share the household tasks instead of just helping out. There may also be differences of power within the relationships between couples because one of the couple has more financial, physical or political power. Sociologists such as Young and Willmott take a 'march of progress' view and believe there is now more equality between couples. However, many feminists strongly disagree as they feel that men still dominate the family and that gender roles are still unequal.

Willmott and Young have suggested that increased opportunities for women in work have changed things because women have become less financially dependent on their husbands. If women are at work they can't do all the household chores on their own and husbands begin to share the chores. Man-Yee Kun found women who earned more did less housework the more they earned. However, many feminist sociologists believe that employment has meant that women actually have more work to do, outside and inside the home, this is called the 'dual burden'. Women's work is just expanding to do paid work, domestic work and emotional work. Gershuny found that wives who worked full time still did 73% of the housework.

Because of the increased number of women at work, the idea of the 'new man' appeared. This is the idea that a new kind of masculinity has developed where males can now show their feminine side and do more tasks such as childcare and domestic chores, even to be a 'house husband'. Although men do now seem to take a more active role in housework, feminists say this is exaggerated by the media and studies have shown that men help out with the more interesting chores such as cooking and taking the children out, but don't do the harder and dirtier jobs. Radical feminists argue that women actually do a 'triple shift', taking on 'emotion work' in supporting the family expressively and caring for other family members – as well as working and doing household chores, but this kind of emotion work is not done by men.

This is related to the fact that society is becoming more child-centred so many fathers now take a more active role in the upbringing of their children and get fulfilment from this. Gray found that men now want quality time with their children and see fatherhood as important.

Another factor that has affected the domestic division of labour in the family is the increased help from technology in the home, such as washing machines, which have made domestic chores easier. Less time is therefore spent carrying out these tasks. However Sclater disagrees because technology has changed the way the chores are done but not necessarily made fewer chores. Machines that are supposed to make domestic chores easier actually produce more work. This is because the level of cleanliness and diet expected is higher, ☞

A very good opening paragraph that shows understanding of both the concepts in the question – domestic division of labour and power – and suggests that there may have been some changes in relationships in recent years. This has also been related to different theoretical perspectives.

A relevant factor – the increase in women's employment – is identified and its effect is analysed. Evidence is provided and feminist views presented as evaluation. The paragraph is clear and relevant – all skills are in evidence here.

Another factor – the 'new man' – is introduced, explained and related to the question. This is criticized from a feminist point of view. The concept of the 'triple shift' is explained.

Some repetition, but the relevance of child-centredness and changing fatherhood is shown and explained, though this is not discussed in detail.

The factor of increased technology in the home is examined, plus the commercialization of housework. This concept is evaluated and evidence supplied for both sides of the argument.

These two paragraphs turn to the other issue in the question and therefore show good interpretation and application. The issue of power is identified in differential earnings, decision-making and physical differences. However, there is limited analysis of these factors.

The final paragraph provides a good conclusion and refers back to the wording of the question. It brings together some of the arguments cited, but also summarizes the theoretical perspectives and suggests that it is hard to determine how far things have changed.

so that women have to spend a longer amount of time doing domestic duties. However, Silver and Schor suggest that the burden of housework has been reduced significantly by the 'commercialization of housework', for example the availability of ready-meals.

In many couples there are important differences in power. This may affect decision-making for the family, and how resources are divided. The most important factor here is earnings. Pahl and Vogler found that pooling of incomes was more common where couples both work full time. If only the husband worked, or the wife worked part time, the husband had more control over the money. Edgell found that wives tended to only be in charge of minor household decisions. The main reason for these differences is that men are likely to earn more, so women are more dependent.

The other factor that affects power relations is physical power. Radical feminists look at widespread domestic violence and say that this is evidence of patriarchy. They also say that patriarchy does not operate just because men have more muscle-power than women, but because men control the streets, the courts and the police.

So there are many factors such as women in paid employment, and advances in technology that have affected the domestic division of labour and power between couples. The extent to which the division of labour has changed is hard to decide. Some march of progress sociologists see it as becoming more egalitarian, but many feminists still see it as a burden for women, with higher expectations and more work.

Overall, this is a very good answer. There is plenty of evidence of sociological knowledge and understanding of the material. It is conceptually detailed and provides plenty of appropriate evidence.

There is a clear rationale in the organisation of the essay. Each part of the question is dealt with. Different factors are taken in turn and are explained. Some discussion and evaluation is then provided for each. Throughout the essay there is frequent reference made to the question set and to sociological perspectives. The idea that relationships between couples are changing is taken up as a theme and applied to each factor discussed – an outline of how might things have changed, followed by some evidence that things have not changed so much after all.

The essay deals both with the domestic division of labour and with power. The latter is only given two paragraphs, but several points are covered. For top marks, both aspects of such a question MUST be covered, but they do not have to be covered absolutely equally. Here there is enough on power, but it could be developed more effectively. The role of earnings, decision-making and domestic violence could be discussed more fully. ☞

Other issues that could be included might be the growth of same-sex couples and their relationships, social class and ethnic differences, the impact of feminism and kin networks. Evaluation might be developed through different perspectives, such as postmodernism, or by considering the relative importance of different factors.

Mark 21/24

The final part of this answer continues on the next two pages

This is a good opening paragraph, introducing the functionalist view of the family and using material from the Item.

A functionalist sociologist is identified and two points of theory are described: family universality and the different functions the family performs. These points are explained well.

Analysis and evaluation of Murdock's theory is developed and it is compared with another perspective.

Another functionalist is introduced and his views on the functions of the family are explained well, with some analysis. An evaluative point is added.

Another aspect of Parson's work, on family roles, is appropriately explained and criticized from a feminist point of view, using several more concepts.

05 *Using material from Item 1B and elsewhere, assess the contribution of functionalist theories to an understanding of the family.* [**24 marks**]

Functionalists believe that all social institutions serve a function for society and provide society with stability. Many functionalists see the family as the institution that does this through teaching children the values and norms of the society. Item B shows how the functionalists view the family as a 'vital social institution' which 'carries out a number of essential functions, both for individuals and for society as whole'.

The functionalist sociologist Murdock claimed that the nuclear family is found in every society because it performs four main functions that are essential to the existence of society and no other institution can perform. The four functions are reproductive, sexual, educational and economic. Murdock said that the reproductive function was vital for society to survive; he saw the family as the best place for reproduction to take place. Similarly, he believed that the sexual function should take place within the family, because if sex is controlled by keeping it in the family it helps maintain stability and it binds the couple together rather than having a free for all. Murdock saw education as an important function for the family. The family socializes children into society's values and norms. The final function Murdock identified was the economic one. The family provides for its members' basic needs, such as food and shelter.

Other sociologists have criticized Murdock's view of the family because it only sees the family as nuclear. There are many family structures such as extended, lone-parent, gay, reconstituted that are not included. This view that a nuclear family set up is the best for raising children means he is saying that there's right and wrong families and ways of bringing up children. Some interpretivist sociologists say that there may be lots of different family structures because of cultural differences, but that doesn't make them wrong.

Another functionalist sociologist is Talcott Parsons. Parsons believed that the family has two main functions. The first is the primary socialization of children, in which the family teaches children the society's culture and its shared values and norms. It also prepares them for life in society and the world of work. The second function the family performs, Parsons says, is the stabilization of adult personalities. In the family, adults can relax away from work in a loving environment. This is referred to as the 'warm bath theory'. Steel and Kidd describe adults as being themselves and letting themselves go in a childish and undignified way. This is the idea that the family acts as a safety valve, getting rid of the stresses of the workplace, and Parsons says it is important to keep the economy going. Parsons is often criticized for producing a picture of the family that is too harmonious and rosy. He doesn't take account of things like domestic violence and child abuse.

Parsons is also criticized by feminists for his views on gender roles. He argues that there must be two different roles within the family, to perform the functions satisfactorily. The male must take an 'instrumental' role as the breadwinner and the female must take the 'expressive role' as the carer and home-maker. This is criticized by feminists because it is patriarchy. It sees the woman's role as housewife and the man as dominant. Feminists reject this idea that the roles are natural – this division of labour doesn't happen everywhere and it only benefits men. 👉

Functionalists are criticized by Marxists, who say that the family does not function for its members and all society, but really helps capitalism. The things that the family does benefit the ruling class, not the ordinary people. This is because it gives workers lots of family responsibilities, so that they are less likely to strike. The warm bath at home helps them to cope with long hours of boring hard work outside. Also the family trains up for free the new generation of the workforce for capitalism and teaches them to work hard and be obedient. Finally, the members of the family buy lots of consumer goods from shops and this helps to keep the capitalist system going.

Feminists also criticize the functionalist view of the family. They say that it functions mainly to benefit men because it supports a patriarchal view of women. Marxist feminists argue that it is the women who provide the emotional warm bath to absorb men's anger and frustration, so they are the ones that suffer. Fran Ansley calls women the 'takers of shit'. Women are also seen as a reserve army of labour, they are mostly in the housewife role but they can be called up when they are needed to work in the economy and then sacked when they are not needed any more. So this just benefits capitalism.

In conclusion the functionalist theory of the family helps us to understand how important it is in society and all the different things that the family functions to do for its members. However, many other sociologists say this view is out of date and is too rosy, they only focus on the good role that the family performs. Marxists say the family functions to help the capitalists and feminists see it as benefiting men by oppressing women. Other sociologists argue that the functionalist view does not take enough account of family variation and change.

A good paragraph, with a range of points made. An alternative perspective, Marxism, is contrasted with the functionalist point of view. Several points of the functionalist approach are successfully interpreted from this alternative perspective. This is a development of the point in Item 1B, so it would be useful to identify it as such.

Feminist criticisms of functionalist theory are put forward effectively and several more sociological concepts are used.

This is a good conclusion. Both positive and negative criticism is included plus a general summary of the main arguments. Points from the Item are brought into the conclusion but not identified.

Overall this is a good answer. It shows a good level of sociological knowledge and understanding. Throughout the essay there is evidence of analysis, in that concepts and ideas are explained and discussed. Material from the Item is used.

The answer could be improved by addressing the question more closely. The question asks for an assessment of functionalism's contribution to understanding the family, so more reference should be made to this in particular. For example, it would be a good way to focus the conclusion. The answer uses material from the Item at several points; it's always a good idea to make sure the examiner realizes where this is done – if a question asks for the use of an Item, then it's essential to do this to achieve top marks.

The discussion of functionalism is restricted to two theorists, though these are well presented. There are other aspects of Parsons' work in particular that could be included, for example on 'functional fit'. The continuation of some functionalist ideas by the New Right could be mentioned, plus the postmodernist views of family choice and diversity.

Mark: 20/24

Total marks: 2 + 4 + 6 + 21 + 20 = 53/60 = grade A

Families and Households (sample exam paper 2)

Read Items 2A and 2B below and answer parts (01) to (05) that follow.

Item 2A

In recent decades, there have been significant changes in patterns of marriage in Britain. In the past, the patriarchal family was based on the belief that marriage was essential and was expected to last for life. Today people are getting married later, the number of first marriages has fallen, and more people get divorced.

Item 2B

The commonly held view of children today is that they are different from adults, in terms of both biological and psychological development. Children know much less about the world; they are vulnerable and need protection.

However, this has not always been the way children have been viewed. In the past, children were seen very differently and were expected to work from a young age. It was only gradually that children were excluded from many occupations and the age at which they could start work was raised. This suggests that childhood is socially constructed.

Questions

01 Explain what is meant by the 'patriarchal' family (**Item 2A**, line 2).
[**2 marks**]

02 Suggest **two** effects of the decrease in the death rate in the last hundred years. [**4 marks**]

03 Suggest **three** reasons why people are now marrying at a later age (**Item 2A**). [**6 marks**]

04 Examine the extent of, and reasons for, family and household diversity in Britain today. [**24 marks**]

05 Using material from **Item 2B** and elsewhere, assess the view that childhood is socially constructed. [**24 marks**]

Grade C answer

01 *Explain what is meant by the 'patriarchal' family.* [**2 marks**]

> The patriarchal family essentially refers to a family that is male dominated. For example, in the majority of families men make all the most important decisions such as buying a new car, whereas women make minor decisions such as what to have for meals. This shows that the family is 'patriarchal'.

The concept is correctly explained as 'male dominated'. The rest of the answer is unnecessary as the candidate has already answered the question. This time could be better spent elsewhere. However, if the example of decision-making was the only information offered, this would gain 1 mark as an example of patriarchy, but not an explanation.
Mark 2/2

02 *Suggest two effects of the decrease in the death rate in the last hundred years.* [**4 marks**]

> One effect of the decrease in the death rate in the past 100 years is that more care is needed for the elderly, as there are more living to an older age. This care can come either from relatives or health clinics, and has meant a change in how the elderly are viewed in our society, with many now viewing them as a burden on the taxpayer, who invariably has to fund their health (through the NHS). This has led to many attaching a negative stigma to the aged, thus ignoring the benefits which an ageing society can undoubtedly bring.
>
> This leads us on to the other effect by the decreasing death rate, which is a positive one. Since old people are now more likely to stay healthy and fit for a longer period of time, it can be argued that they form a vital part of the 'voluntary workforce' (childcare for grandchildren), whilst also providing good role-models for young children. Indeed sociologists Ginn and Arber found in their study on old people that they could play an invaluable role in society which is often forgotten, although they admitted that it was often working class individuals on low pay who made up the bulk of this 'voluntary workforce'.

Two appropriate effects are suggested: more care is needed for the elderly as there are more living to an older age; people are now staying fit for longer and so can act as a voluntary workforce. There are two other possible answers here: the growing burden on the taxpayer and the negative stigma of ageism. Again, there is more detail in this answer than is required.

Other appropriate answers might refer to pensions, the labour market, beanpole families or the positive aspects of retirement.
Mark 4/4

03 *Suggest three reasons why people are now marrying at a later age.* **[6 marks]**

In recent years British society has become much more secular, so it's now seen as ok to live together before getting married, so people get married later, after a period of cohabitation.

Many women now want to be more than a housewife and mother, so many choose to pursue a career before settling down and getting married, so therefore there's a later marriage age in general.

Another reason why people are marrying later is because there is more divorce.

Two appropriate reasons are suggested: British society is more secular, so there is less stigma attached to cohabitation; many women wish to pursue a career first. The point about divorce needs to be developed, for example to suggest that the fear of divorce makes couples wait longer before marriage to try to make sure their marriage will last.

Other reasons could be: more educational opportunities; the rising cost of weddings and house-buying; the increased availability of contraception (so fewer 'shotgun' weddings).
Mark 4/6

04 *Examine the extent of, and reasons for, family and household diversity in Britain today.* **[24 marks]**

Family diversity refers to the range of different family structures and types, which many believe to be increasing. Traditionally, the family structure is 'nuclear'. However recently many more family structures have become more common for a variety of reasons.

One of the main reasons for more diversity is the divorce rate. This has led to more lone-parent and reconstituted families. The New Right argue that this is bad for society and has led to a lot of social problems like juvenile delinquency, because boys no longer have male role models in the family and turn to peer groups and gangs.

There is a lot of evidence to suggest that family structure is becoming more diverse. Berthoud argued that there was cultural diversity (the different groups in society and the way they construct families), and that each ethnic group can be placed on a line of continuum between old fashioned values and modern individualism. The wide range of groups within British society shows that the society has more tolerance of different ethnic subcultures, although white British people make up 85% of the population. This suggests that cultural diversity has been exaggerated a lot.

Sexual diversity is also now more common within British society, due to less homophobia against gay and lesbian couples. Gay couples have also recently been given the right to civil partnerships (in 2005), and are in many ways ☞

The meaning of diversity is explained. It would be useful to suggest some types of diversity here.

Divorce is cited as a reason for increased diversity, but its importance is not discussed. There is a chance missed here for some good analysis. The focus of the second sentence is on the consequences rather than the reasons for diversity.

This paragraph adds little to the answer, though there is some potentially relevant material here. Ethnic cultural diversity in families is referred to, but there is minimal focus on the family.

now seen as equal to traditional nuclear families. However gay couples still make up less than 5% of all couples, whilst the nuclear family accounts for 39% of the population.

There is also evidence of household diversity as well as in families. Single-person households are becoming more common. One reason is that there are more old people living alone because of increased life expectancy. The increasing divorce rate within British society has also meant that many people live alone, but this is while in between relationships, rather than as a long-term choice. One study found that in an 11-year period just 7% of people were living alone throughout the whole period, so for most people living in a single-person household is temporary not permanent; most would still like to be in a nuclear family. There is an increasing number of couples who cohabit rather than live in marriage, probably as a result of a general lack of stigma (which comes from the secularization of our society).

Overall, it is clear that diversity within British society in both the family and households has increased. We now live in a multi-cultural society, there is less stigma about sexual diversity and single-person and cohabiting households are increasingly common. However despite this, a nuclear family is still the most common form of household, and cultural and sexual diversity is still limited. Most people say they want to live in nuclear families.

Overall this answer shows reasonable knowledge and understanding. However, only three types of families/households are described – gay and lesbian couples, single-person households and cohabiting couples – plus there is unfocused mention of cultural diversity and other family types. However, the answer does deal with households as well as families.

Several reasons are included – divorce, cultural differences, gay couples, increased life expectancy, increased cohabitation rates – and several references to the extent of diversity. However, a closer focus on the words in the question – 'reasons for and extent of' – would improve marks for interpretation and application. There are several brief items of analysis and evaluation in the answer, but more evidence of these skills would be useful. There are some relevant sociological concepts used.

Other types of families/households that could be discussed would be lone parents, reconstituted families, extended families, beanpole families, divorce-extended families, shared households of single people, etc. One way of organizing the essay structure would be to use a typology such as that put forward by the Rapoports. It is important to deal with both parts of the question asked – answers should include analysis of both the reasons for diversity AND the extent of diversity. This answer does cover both to a certain extent. More reference could be made to sociological sources and perspectives on family diversity, such as New Right, feminist and postmodern approaches.

Mark 15/24

A good paragraph. One type of diversity – gay and lesbian couples – is appropriately explained and reasons given for this diversity. There is also a reference to the extent of this diversity in the final sentence, which gives a point of evaluation.

This is a good paragraph, focusing on households rather than families, and single-person households in particular. Two reasons are given for the increase of these households. There is some good analysis and evaluation, supported by evidence. Finally, another type of diversity, cohabiting couples, is cited and a reason given for their increase. However, the presentation is rather superficial and there is potential here for further analysis.

This is mainly repetition; little more is added. There is a good evaluative point in the last sentence; this could be developed much more effectively using Chester, for example.

A partially successful attempt to explain what is meant by 'socially constructed', this shows some understanding of the concept but fuller explanation could be included.

This paragraph has potential but is too superficial. It would be useful to analyze the ways in which children were seen differently in the past, perhaps based on the work of Ariès. The reasons for the changes in childhood could also be analyzed. The second part of the paragraph refers to cultural rather than time differences, but again is rather thin. The issue of class and/or status is raised but not used.

There is a brief reference to childhood in Britain today, but then this paragraph returns to the question of cultural differences. The writer correctly links this point to the question and the Item. At this point a discussion of the nature of childhood today in the UK could be usefully included.

This paragraph contains some analysis and two points of evaluation. An alternative point of view is outlined and that view is then criticized.

This paragraph is mainly repetition of material. Little more is added to the answer.

05 *Using material from Item 2B and elsewhere, assess the view that childhood is socially constructed.* [**24 marks**]

It is generally accepted within sociology that 'nurture' is the most important aspect of our socialization and so it is to be expected that childhood differs from culture to culture, thus making it socially constructed.

One way in which childhood can be seen to be socially constructed is reflected in Item B, where it states that children have in the past been seen 'very differently'. For example, in the 19th century children were expected to work in mines and factories from a very early age. In modern society this is unthinkable to us now, which shows that childhood is socially constructed as it has changed dramatically over time. Childhood is also related to social class. For example, working class children in India may have to do hard manual work to add to the family's income but the son of the maharajah would be waited upon hand and foot by servants.

If we look at childhood across varying cultures, there's also evidence that childhood is socially constructed. Britain today is child-centred, and a child is not seen as capable of looking after themselves until they are at least 16. This can be very different in other cultures, such as for poor children in developing countries where they may have to look after younger siblings before they get to the age of 10. This clearly shows that childhood cannot be defined the same for everybody as it is different according to the culture. So it is therefore socially constructed.

However we could argue that all very young children, no matter where or when they are living, are helpless and completely dependent in the first few years of life. This is the argument put forward by socio-biologists like Wilson and Dawkins, who believe that childhood is determined by biology. However, this theory has flaws because the way childhood is seen in any society is determined by the adults who have the power, so it must be socially constructed. So in any society, how childhood is seen depends on power.

To conclude, it would appear that childhood is almost certainly 'socially constructed'. The meaning that is given to childhood in different societies past and present makes it very difficult to argue otherwise. Socio-biologists have attempted to do so, arguing that childhood is 'biologically determined', but as we have seen there is considerable evidence against this view, suggesting that such theorists are misguided and should not be given too much credibility.

The answer has shown knowledge and understanding of social construction and has identified some ways in which childhood is socially constructed by comparing childhood over time and between cultures. However, these have not been well explained or discussed. Several other points about social construction are hinted at but not developed. For example, the points about past and other societies could be contrasted with a discussion of the modern notion of childhood and an examination of the factors that led to its development. Concepts such as child-centredness, 'toxic childhood', the education system, the commercialization of childhood, the influence of the mass media, age patriarchy, gender and class differences could be explored. Some material from the Item has been used.

The answer includes some brief analysis and evaluation via biological determinism. Further analysis and evaluation could be shown by discussing different views on the status of childhood today, such as child protection, child liberation, globalization and/or the 'disappearance' of childhood.

Some of the time spent on questions 01 and 02 could have been used to gain more marks here.

Mark 12/24

Total marks: 2 + 4 + 4 + 15 + 12 = 37/60 = grade C

Improving your grade

The following examples show how you can improve your answers to the short questions for Families and Households.

---

01 *Explain what is meant by the term 'expressive' role.* [**2 marks**]

There is some knowledge shown here but there is no explanation of what an expressive role is. Using the term to explain itself is not helpful!
Mark 0/2

> **Weak answer**
>
> The expressive role is an idea put forward by functionalist Talcott Parsons. It says that women are naturally expressive, but men have an instrumental role.

Housework is not expressive, but 'childcare' involves the notion of nurturing and care. However, it is still only an example, not an explanation. – 1 mark
Mark 1/2

> **Better answer**
>
> This is the role of housework and childcare that is usually given to women.

The expressive role has been correctly explained as the caring and nurturing role. Note that the word 'role' is not included in the inverted commas in the question, so does not need to be explained.
Mark 2/2

> **Good answer**
>
> The expressive role is perceived to be the caring and nurturing role in the family. Functionalists see it as the woman's role.

---

02 *Explain the difference between a family and a household.* [**4 marks**]

The two terms have been confused. Members of a family do not necessarily live together and a family is more than a group of people. However, an example of a family is given. – 1 mark

A household is not a place. – 0 marks
Mark 1/4

> **Weak answer**
>
> A family is a group of people that live together (e.g. parents and their children). A household is the place where people live.

The first sentence gives an example of a family rather than a definition or explanation. – 1 mark ☞

> **Better answer**
>
> There are many types of family, but it usually consists of two parents and children known as a nuclear family. A household involves people living together and they can be related or unrelated.

Household is explained correctly. – 2 marks
Mark 3/4

Good answer

A family is a group of people who are related by blood or marriage. A household is a group of people who live in the same dwelling (though it may be just one person).

This is a good answer, explaining both terms correctly. It is clear and concise.
Mark 4/4

03 *Suggest two reasons why there has been an increase in one-person households.* [**4 marks**]

Weak answer

When people move about the country to get jobs, they often live on their own for a while.

Another reason is that women live longer than men, the average is 85 for women and 75 for men. So many widows live alone after their husbands have died.

The first answer correctly identifies geographical mobility as a possible reason, but includes no notion of increase or change. – 1 mark

The second answer also does not show why things have changed, or why this would lead to an increase in one-person households. To get full marks, an answer would need to refer to increased life expectancy to explain the increase in the number of widows. – 1 mark
Mark 2/4

Better answer

One reason for the increase in one-person households is that mothers tend to get custody of children after divorce, so the divorced husband lives on his own.

Another reason is that today women are more financially independent than in the past and feel they can live alone to follow their careers.

The first answer contains no notion of change or increase, but correctly identifies divorce as a reason. – 1 mark

The second answer correctly points to the increase in women following careers. – 2 marks
Mark 3/4

Good answer

One reason for the increase in one-person households is because today it's more accepted for a person to move out of home to live alone. In the past they would only move out when they got married.

Another reason is that there has been an increase in divorce rates, so there are more spouses moving out who need to find somewhere to live on their own.

Both answers given are appropriate and both show that there has been an increase. – 4 marks
Mark 4/4

Families and Households

Absolute poverty	Lacking the resources to pay for the basic necessities of life such as food, shelter, basic health care and warmth
Achieved status	A position in society which affects the way others view you that is earned at least partly through your own efforts, e.g. a job
Adultist	Biased in favour of the interests or viewpoints of adults at the expense of children
Ageing population	A situation in which an increasing proportion of the population in a given country is middle aged or older
Alienation	A sense of being distanced from something so that it feels alien, e.g. feeling a lack of connection and fulfilment in work
Apollonian image of the child	Sees children as being born good but requiring the good aspects of their nature to be coaxed out of them sympathetically
Ascribed status	A position in society which affects the way others view you that is given by birth, e.g. being male or female
Beanpole family	A family in which links between generations, i.e. between grandparents, parents and grandchildren, are strong but links with other relations such as aunts, uncles and cousins are weak
Birth rate	The number of live births per thousand of the population per year
Black feminism	A version of **feminism** which argues that racial/**ethnic** differences between women are very important
Bourgeoisie	The **ruling class** in **capitalism** who own property such as capital, businesses and shares
Breadwinner	The person doing all or most of the paid work in order to pay for the expenses of a family
Capitalist society/ capitalism	A society in which people are employed for wages, and businesses are set up with the aim of making a profit
Cereal packet image of the family	The image of the family often presented in marketing as a conventional heterosexual **nuclear family** of legally married couples with one or more (but not too many) children, with a male **breadwinner** and a female housewife
Child-centred	A situation in which the interests of children are put before the interests of adults
Chosen families	Groups of people who are treated like and seen as family members even when they are not related by blood or marriage; friends can be members of chosen families
Chronological age	The number of years since you were born
Civil partnership	A legal partnership of two people, whether homosexual or heterosexual, with similar rights and responsibilities to a marriage
Class/social class	Groups within society distinguished by their economic position and who are therefore unequal, e.g. the middle class in better paid non-manual jobs and the working class in less well-paid physical jobs
Cohabitation/ cohabiting	Living together in an intimate relationship without being married
Competition	When individuals or businesses try to do better than one another, e.g. in selling more goods than another company

Confluent love	Love that is dependent upon partners benefiting from the relationship rather than on unconditional devotion
Conjugal roles	The roles of husband and wife within marriage (it may also be applied to male and female partners who cohabit but are not married)
Death rate	The number of people dying per thousand of the population per year
Deconstruction	The process where something breaks down or is taken apart for the purpose of analysis
De-differentiation	A decline in the importance of differences between things, e.g. a decline in the importance of differences between age groups
Demographic revolution	A situation in which fertility rates and death rates decline as people come to expect lower rates of infant mortality and therefore have fewer children
Dependency ratio	The number of people in non-economically active age groups (children and the retired) relative to the size of the population of working age
Developmentalism	The view that childhood consists of a series of stages in which children develop progressively
Difference feminism	Feminism which emphasizes that the position of women in society varies and women cannot be seen as a single, united group
Dionysian image of the child	Sees children as pursuing their own desires, which can lead to them acting in evil ways
Disengagement	The gradual withdrawal of people from social roles, e.g. older people when they retire
Division of labour	The way in which jobs are divided up between two or more people, e.g. who does particular tasks in a household
Dispersed extended family	Kin who keep in touch with one another but are geographically spread out
Diversity	Variety in social life
Divorce	The legal ending of a marriage
Divorce rate	The number of people who divorce per thousand married people in a population per year
Domestic abuse	Actions which are damaging to current or former partners in an intimate relationship; this can include physical, sexual, emotional or financial abuse
Domestic labour	Work done within the home such as housework and childcare, it may be unpaid but it creates value just as paid work does
Domestic violence	Actions involving the use of force or the threat of force against current or former partners in an intimate relationship which are harmful to the other partner. Domestic violence need not take place within the home but can take place anywhere
Dominant framework	The most widely held and commonsense view of the difference between childhood and adulthood which sees them as opposites and believes that children have not yet attained the key characteristics necessary for them to become full persons
Dual-earner families	Families in which both partners are in paid employment

Dysfunctional families	Families which do not function well for family members or in fulfilling social roles, e.g. they fail to socialize children adequately
Economic base	In Marxist theory the foundation of society consisting of the economic system
Economic function	The role the family plays in providing food, shelter and the ability to consume products for its members
Educational function	The role of the family in providing a stable environment in which children can be socialized into the culture of their society
Emotion work	The time and effort involved thinking about and acting to produce the emotional well-being and happiness of others
Empty-shell marriage	A marriage where the partners continue to live together but the emotional attachment and sexual relationship have come to an end
Ethnic group	A group within a population regarded by themselves or by others as culturally distinctive; they usually see themselves as having a common geographic origin
Extended family	The family wider than the nuclear family. As well as parents and children it includes other relatives such as aunts, uncles and grandparents
Extended kinship network	The interrelationships between people related by blood or marriage regardless of whether they live together
Familistic gender regimes	Sets of government policies which support traditional **nuclear families** in which husbands are the main breadwinner and wives do most of the domestic work
Family diversity	The growth of variety in the structure and nature of family types
Female career-core	According to Sheeran, the most basic family unit consisting of a mother and child/children
Female-headed family	Family with a female head of household, usually without an adult male
Feminism	Theory of society which claims that women are disadvantaged and exploited by men, while men are dominant and run society in their own interests
Fertility rate	The number of live births per thousand women aged 15 to 44 per year
Free-market	A system in which businesses can compete with one another without state interference
Friendship networks	Groups of friends who interact with one another without living together
Functionalism	A belief that social institutions serve some positive purpose
Function	A useful job performed by an institution for society
Gay and lesbian households	Households based around male partners or female partners in an intimate, sexual relationship
Gender regimes	Sets of policies which make assumptions about the roles of men and women in family life
Gender roles	The socially expected behaviour of men and women in a particular society
Geographical mobility	The movements of people to different regions or countries
Heteronorm	The belief that all sexually intimate relationships should be based on heterosexuality
Household	A group of people who share the same accommodation
Identity	The way people are seen by themselves or others in society

Ideological state apparatus	According to Poulantzas, parts of society which encourage people to accept the values favoured by the **ruling class** and which help to maintain **capitalist** society
Ideology	A distorted set of beliefs which favours the interests of a particular social group
Illegitimacy	Children born to unmarried parents
Individualism	An emphasis upon the desires or interests of individual people rather than those of wider social groups
Individualistic gender regimes	Sets of social policies which do not assume that husbands and wives will follow traditional roles and which accommodate the choices made by individuals regardless of whether they are male or female
Individualization	A process in which the wishes of individuals are seen as more important than the maintenance of traditional norms and values, and the prioritization of the interests of individuals above those of social groups
Industrialization	The process whereby manufacturing takes over from agriculture as the most important component in a society's economy
Infant mortality rate	The number of children dying before their first birthday per thousand of live births per year
Intergenerational	Between generations, e.g. between parents and children
Intragenerational	Within a generation, e.g. brothers and sisters
Isolated nuclear family	A **nuclear family** (parents and children) which is relatively self-sufficient and has few contacts with extended kin
Joint conjugal roles	Relationships between husbands and wives in which both do some paid work and both do housework and provide childcare. Typically with this type of role, men and women spend a good deal of time together
Kibbutz	A small communal settlement in Israel
Kin	People linked by blood or marriage
Kinship networks	Interrelationships between people related by blood or marriage whether or not they live together
Late modernity	According to Giddens, the most recent phase in the development of **modernity**
Liberal feminism	A version of **feminism** which is relatively moderate and believes that the position of women in society can be improved through reform rather than radical or revolutionary change
Life course	The development and change in people's lives over periods of time. Unlike life-cycle the life course does not have fixed and predictable stages
Life-cycle	The stages of life, e.g. childhood, young adulthood and old age, which are predictable and assumed to be experienced in the same way by different people
Life expectancy	The average age to which a particular group of people is likely to live
Lone parent family	Family consisting of one parent living with one or more of their children
Malestream	To **feminists**, something which is mainstream and male-dominated or biased in favour of men
Marital breakdown	The ending of a marriage whether through **divorce**, **separation** or the development of an **empty-shell marriage**

Masculinity	The behaviour and social roles expected of men in a particular culture
Matrifocal family	A family headed by the mother where she is not co-resident with a male partner
Means of production	Those things required to produce goods such as land, machinery, capital, technical knowledge and workers
Median	The middle value in any group, e.g. the median age is the age of the person in a population where half of the people are older than them and half are younger
Media-saturated society	A society in which people's impression of reality is largely shaped by high levels of exposure to the mass media
Metanarrative	A 'big story' about how the world works and how people should live their lives, e.g. a political theory or a religion
Middle class	People who have white-collar jobs which require some qualifications and are generally better paid than **working class** jobs
Migration	People leaving or entering a country or area to live for a significant time
Modern	Characteristic of or belonging to modernity
Modernity	An era in the development of society characterized by rationality, i.e. planning to achieve goals, and in which the influence of tradition and religion is reduced compared with previous eras
Mode of production	A system of producing things which dominates society, e.g. **capitalism**
Nayar	Members of a society in southern India
Neo-conventional family	A traditional nuclear family, but one in which both the husband and wife do paid work rather than having a single, male **breadwinner**
Net migration	The difference between the numbers entering and leaving a country (to live for some time rather than just going on holiday)
New reproductive technologies	Technologies which allow previously infertile couples or individuals to have children, e.g. in vitro fertilization (test-tube babies)
New Right	Politicians, thinkers and writers who support the free market rather than state intervention and who believe that traditional moral values should be preserved
Norms	Specific, informal rules of behaviour in a particular society
Nuclear family	A co-resident family of two generations: parents and children
Organizational diversity	Variety in the structure of families, e.g. **lone parent**, **nuclear** and **extended**
Patriarchy/patriarchal	Literally 'rule by the father', usually used by **feminists** to refer to a system in which men have more **power** than women and shape how societies run
Peer group	A group of people with a similar **status** and often age to whom you compare yourself and who may exercise influence on your behaviour
Personal age	How old a person feels rather them how old they actually are
Plastic sexuality	Behaviour where sex can be for pleasure as well as for conceiving children
Population pyramid	A bar chart representing the distribution of the population in different age groups
Pluralization of lifestyles	A process in which people come to live in more varied ways rather than sharing similar ways of living
Post-industrial	The phase of society when manufacturing was the dominant part of the economy

Postmodernity/ postmodern	The era following modernity in which rationality becomes less important, image becomes more important and in which many old social divisions break down
Poverty	Lacking the resources to pay for the minimum acceptable lifestyle
Power	The ability of a person to get their own way or to determine outcomes regardless of the wishes of others
Pre-industrial society	Societies that existed before industrialization where most production was based upon agriculture
Primary relationships	The most important and emotionally charged personal relationships, e.g. between parents and children
Primary socialization	The first stage of the process through which children learn the culture of their society. This takes place in the family
Private enterprise	Businesses owned by individuals or shareholders rather than run by the state
Pull factors	Factors attracting international migrants to move to a particular country
Push factors	Factors encouraging international emigrants to leave a particular country
Radical feminism	The most extreme version of **feminism** which tends to see society as being completely dominated by men and sees the interests of men and women as being very different
Rationality	Behaviour which is geared towards achieving specified goals rather than based on emotion
Reconstituted family	A family that includes members from previous families which have broken up but which come together as two new partners form a relationship
Reflexive project of self	The way individuals constantly think about improving their own lives and developing their identity in contemporary society
Relative poverty	Lacking the resources to pay for a lifestyle which is deemed the minimum acceptable when compared with other people in a particular society at a particular time
Reproductive function	The function of the family in ensuring children are reproduced to enable the survival of society
Ruling class	In Marxist theory, the group who are dominant in society by virtue of their wealth and power
Sandbanham husband	In Nayar society, a visiting husband, usually a warrior. Each woman can have several of these husbands
Secularization	The process whereby religious thinking and religious institutions lose social significance
Separation	A couple living apart without getting divorced Some separations are legal and formal, but most are not
Sexual function	The function of the family in controlling sexual behaviour through monogamy
Single-person household	A person living on their own
Social construction	A behaviour or practice which is produced by society even though it may seem natural or biological
Social mobility	The movement of people between social groups, especially social classes

Socialization	The process through which a person learns the culture of their society
Stabilization of adult personalities	To Parsons, the role of the family in maintaining the psychological health of adults by providing warmth and security and allowing them to act out childish elements in their personality
Status	The amount of esteem in which people are held by others in society
Stepfamily	A family which includes one or more children from a previous relationship
Subject class	In Marxist theory, the group in society who are dominated by the **ruling class** whom they have to work for because they lack the property to produce goods for themselves. The subject class are exploited by the **ruling class**
Superstructure	In Marxist theory, the non-economic parts of society such as the family which are shaped by the economy and controlled by the **ruling class**
Surplus value	Profits made by the **ruling class**
Surrogate motherhood	Where a woman gives birth to a child even though the child is not her genetic offspring (through in vitro fertilization)
Symmetrical family	A family in which both husband and wife do paid employment and both do some housework and provide childcare
Tali husband	In **Nayar** society, a husband who does not live with his wife or have a significant relationship with her
Triple shift	According to Duncombe and Marsden, the three types of work which create a burden for women: paid work, domestic work and **emotion work**
Underclass	The lowest social class, below the rest of the class structure, often seen as consisting of those reliant upon state benefits
Universal	Found in all societies
Values	General beliefs about what is right or wrong in a particular society
Visiting relationship	A relationship where an adult has a partner but they do not live together
Welfare state	Agencies run or financed by the government to provide for the well-being of members of society, such as education, the health service and social services
Working class	People who do manual jobs which require relatively few qualifications and are usually less well-paid than **middle-class** jobs

absolute poverty 63
abuse 12, 50–1
achieved status 7
adultist child image 57
African Caribbean families 35
age categories 45, 66–7
    see also childhood
ageing population 66–7
alienation 9, 12
Apollonian child image 55
Aries, Phillipe 53
ascribed status 7
Asian families 35
asylum seekers 64
attitudinal changes 33, 60–1
beanpole families 19, 28
Beck and Beck-Gernsheim 21, 61
birth parents, surrogacy 31
birth rate 58–61, 66
black feminism 11
border controls 65
bourgeoisie 8–9
breadwinner role 28, 35–6, 46
capitalist society 8–9, 14
cereal packet family image 28
Chester, Robert 36–7
child-centredness 53, 60–1
childcare 46–7
childhood 44, 52–7, 60–1
choice, relationships 42
'chosen families' 13, 31
chronological age 45, 53
civil partnerships 5, 27, 31
class system 8, 11, 18, 22, 25, 30, 45
coalition government, 2010 27
cohabitation 5, 15, 43
    changing patterns 38–9
    diversity 30, 32, 34, 36
    domestic violence 51
cohorts 30, 38
commodities 9
communism 24
competition 14
confluent love 21
conjugal bonds 18
conjugal roles 17, 46–9
construction see social construction
consumption 9, 56
contemporary approach, childhood 56–7
contemporary families 19
conventional approach 57
    see also functionalist theories; New
Right perspectives
conventional families 26, 36–7
    see also nuclear families
culture 30, 34–5, 44
de-differentiation 45
death rate 58, 60, 62–3, 66
decision-making power 48
deconstruction 45
demography 32, 58–67
dependency culture 33
dependency ratio 61, 67
difference feminism 11, 13

Dionysian child image 55
disengagement 67
dispersed extended families 19, 28
diversity 5, 9, 15, 22–3, 27–37
division of labour 30, 46
divorce 21, 26, 30–2, 35–6, 40–3, 51
divorce rates 40
domestic abuse 50–1
domestic labour 9
domestic violence 12, 50–1
dominant framework 52
dual-earner families 26, 30, 60
dysfunctional families 51
economic base 8
economic burden of children 60
economic functions 6
economic systems 8
economic units 42
educational functions 6
emigration 64
emotion work 48–9
emotional intensity 51
empty-shell marriages 40, 41
environmental measures 63
ethnicity 11, 34–5, 37a
extended families
    diversity 28, 35
    domestic violence 51
    relationships 43
    social structures 4–7, 16, 19, 23
families, defining 4–5
familistic gender regimes 25–6
family diversity 5, 9, 15, 27, 28–37
family structure changes 18–19
female carer-core of families 5
feminist theories 9–13, 15–16, 25–6, 45, 51
fertility rate 58–61, 66
fragmentation 36
free-market capitalism 14
friendship networks 31
functionalist theories 4–7, 9, 13–14, 41, 44, 57
gay families 5, 13, 31
gender 22, 25–6, 45–51, 59, 61
gender regimes 25–6
gender roles 22, 49, 59, 61
    see also conjugal roles
genetic parents, surrogacy 31
geographic mobility 6–7, 17, 18
Giddens, Anthony 21, 51, 55
globalization effects 65
government spending 67
health 62–3
heteronorm 31
households 5, 29, 37, 49
housewives 28
housework 46–7
husbands, Nayar people 4
identity 20, 22
ideological differences 5, 11
ideological state apparatus 9
illegitimacy 33
immigration 64
individualism 21, 26, 36, 39, 42, 61

industrial society 6–7, 16–17, 20
inequality 10–11
infant mortality rate 60, 62
infantilization 45
infrastructure 8
inter-/intra-generational links 19
isolated nuclear families 6
Jenks, Christopher 55–6
joint conjugal roles 46
judicial separations 41
kibbutzim 24
kinship networks 6, 18, 22–3, 35, 41, 43, 51
Laslett, Peter 17
late modernity 21
legislation
    divorce 42–3
    migration 65
lesbian families 5, 13, 31, 49
liberal feminism 10–13, 16, 51
life course changes 44–5, 56
life-cycle stages 30, 44–5
life expectancy 44, 62
lifestyle choices 19, 22
living standards 63
lone-parent families 30, 32–5, 36
love 21
male breadwinners 28, 35, 36
malestream views 10, 46
marital breakdown 32, 40–3
marriage 4, 30, 32, 38–43
marriage rates 30, 38–9
Marxist theories 8–13, 45
masculinity 51
matrifocal families 4–5
Mayall, Berry 57
mean divorce rates 40
means of production 8
media-saturated societies 22
median
    age categories 66
    divorce rates 40
medical developments 62
metanarratives 22
middle class 18, 22
migration 34, 58, 64–5
modernity 20–2, 42, 52–5
modes of production 8
money and power 48–9
Murdock, George Peter 4–6
Nayar people 4
neo-conventional families 36–7
net migration 58, 64
New Labour 27
new reproductive technologies 31
New Right perspectives 5, 14–15, 24–5, 27, 51, 56–7
normal chaos of love 21
norms 21, 31
nuclear families
    diversity 28, 35–7
    domestic violence 51
    relationships 41
    social structures 4–6, 14–16, 19, 22, 24–5
nutrition 63

old age 66–7
    see also age categories
operationalizing 41
organizational diversity 30
Parsons, Talcott 6–7, 16–17
party politics 26–7
patriarchal society 10, 25, 46, 51
peer groups 57
personal age 45
plastic sexuality 21
pluralization of lifestyles 19
policies 14, 24–7
political perspectives 24–7
population growth 58
post-industrial society 20, 22
Postman, Neil 54, 56
postmodernist theories 9, 13, 15–16, 20, 22–3, 45, 55
poverty 33, 63, 67
power 46–51
pre-industrial societies 6, 16, 18, 20
primary relationships 55
primary socialization 6
private enterprise 14
proletariat 8
'push/pull' factors, migration 65

radical feminism 10–13, 16, 51
rates
    births 58–61, 66
    deaths 58, 60, 62–3, 66
    divorce 40
    marriage 30, 38–9
rationality 20, 52
reconstituted families 30–1
reflexive project of self 21
relationships 38–45, 55
    see also cohabitation; marriage
relative poverty 63
reproductive functions 6
risk society 21
ruling class 8
secularization 39, 42
segregated conjugal roles 46
separation 32, 35–6, 40, 41
sexual abuse 12
sexual functions 6
sexuality 21
Shorter, Edward 54
single parenthood see lone-parent families
social change 16–19
social class see class system

social construction
    age 45, 67
    childhood 52–3
social mobility 7
social policy see policies
social roles 44
social structures 4–27
socialization 6, 44, 52, 54
spouses, conflict 41–2
    see also marriage
stabilization of adult personalities 6
Stacey, Judith 22
status 7
stepfamilies 30
structural differentiation 7
subject class 8
superstructure 8–9
surrogate motherhood 31
survey research 46
symmetrical families 18, 46
time, conjugal roles 47
underclass 25, 33
universal, families as 4–6
visiting relationships 35
welfare provisions 18, 63
working class 18